HOLOCAUST MEMOIRS OF A BERGEN-BELSEN SURVIVOR

CLASSMATE OF ANNE FRANK

NANETTE BLITZ KONIG

ISBN 9789492371621 (ebook)

ISBN 9789492371614 (paperback)

ISBN 9789493056657 (hardcover)

ISBN 9789493231405 (audiobook)

Publisher: Amsterdam Publishers

Holocaust Memoirs of a Bergen-Belsen Survivor is part of the series Holocaust Survivor Memoirs World War II

Original Portuguese title: Eu Sobrevivi Ao Holocausto, Universo dos Livros, 2015 (ISBN: 9788579308765)

Translator: Rafa Lombardino

CONTENTS

I dedicate this book to my dear parents, Martijn Willem and Helene: I owe my life to you, as well as all the love I have been given and can still feel to this day.

INTRODUCTION

Unfortunately, there is no delete button for the mind. I would like to be able to erase everything I have lived and seen, especially all the suffering. And the suffering was not only inside me—it was outside as well. I could breathe in that suffering; it was part of my world. But then I stop and think, what good would it do to forget it all? What could I have to gain? Peace of mind? Perhaps, but it would have been a fake peace, a blind peace, because I know that forgetting is allowing others to experience the worst of your nightmares. I remember so I can stay alive, because forgetting means dying and losing my family forever.

When remembering the Holocaust, everyone wonders, how did we let this happen? How can human beings be capable of such brutality, such lack of love? I still wonder about it myself, and I believe my family—the one I created after putting myself back together when the War was over—wonders about the exact same thing. Stories from concentration camps bring nightmares to adults as if they were helpless little children.

Stories from concentration camps bring nightmares to adults as if they were helpless little children.

And if adults have trouble processing it all, imagine what it is like for little kids. One of my grandchildren came to me one time and asked me, out of the blue, "Grandma, is it true that the German would give soap bars to Jewish people, pretending they were going to shower, but they actually wanted to kill everybody?" History could never let me be; I am history itself. I took the time to assimilate my grandchild's question. I was paralyzed with fear of making him lose his innocence, but what could I possibly say to him? My grandson needed to know what horror was and that, unfortunately, it is something that can exist. "Yes, it is true," I told him. "That is why we must fight to the end, so that it never happens again." That was when I had to swallow my pride and the bitter memory of a time when living in pain was the only way to be alive.

"So that it never happens again..." Time slips through our fingers. With time, the Holocaust is becoming part of a distant past, but we must keep dragging it back to the present. It is sad, but the world still suffers with so many wars. I will go down fighting for all human beings never to suffer or lose their dignity, as it happened to the Jewish people back then, as it happened to me. The need to tell this story comes from a need to make the world aware of what happened.

I needed to overcome the pain and move on. I had to hold my head up high and talk about the days when I could not even look at members of the so-called "superior race" in the eye. I thought long and hard about the importance of sharing my story, despite how painful it is, but I needed to wait for the right moment, the right person. After some fateful disappointments and frustrated attempts, I welcomed Marcia Batista into my home. She encouraged me to tell these stories and proved to be the ideal partner for this project because, like me, she believes in how important it is to talk about the Holocaust to those who are not familiar with that part of history, to those who do not know enough about it, to those who do not accept it or—worse yet—cannot believe it happened. We thought we needed to make this dark period of world history clearer, no matter how many times it took, so no more lives are wasted by ignorance or intolerance. This is our fight, and this is our legacy.

On these pages, you will read about events that will forever live in my memory, like a movie playing in a loop—events that still haunt my dreams to this day.

My intention with this book is not to invite you to read a story that has a happy ending. I invite you to perhaps experience a future that will bring serenity and harmony. On these pages, you will read about events that will forever live in my memory, like a movie playing in a loop—events that still haunt my dreams to this day. I could never remain silent after all that happened, after all I have lived to tell. The price of freedom is everlasting vigilance. As the Spanish philosopher and poet George Santayana once said, "Those who do not remember the past are condemned to repeat it."

Nanette Bliz Konig (left) and Anne Frank (right) at the Jewish school (Joods Lyceum at Stadstimmertuin) Amsterdam, 1941-42.

1

LIFE BEFORE THE WAR

Can we ever foresee the moment when our lives are about to be turned upside down, when all that is familiar will be no more? Could I ever identify the exact moment when the course of my life would be changed forever? Sometimes I think about my childhood and remember the times I spent with my father, my mother, and my two brothers. These are such distant memories that I have to make a strong effort to prevent those black-and-white images from fading for once and for all. I sometimes wonder whether those days really existed, or if they are part of a fairy tale other people have told me about—maybe a nurse after the war—so that I could recover quickly from those dark moments.

Those pictures remind me that I still have my faculties and, to my relief, I did indeed experience those moments. I pick up a picture and see how happy my parents were on their wedding day. Those were such good moments filled with love, and I am happy I have not forgotten them yet. Childhood reminds me of smiles, laughter, lightness, and liberty. Happy faces so pure that were condemned to in-existence for the simple fact that they were born Jewish. Those are the times that make many of us wonder why we were born this way.

It is not that we do not love who we were; being Jewish was a matter of pride, and we could not be any different. Still, the doubt remains: Why us? Why did they do that to *us*?

Understanding my trajectory means to understand the history of Europe, the history of the world back then. How many millions of lives changed during that period?

Our stories will never be only ours. My story, Nanette's story, is intertwined with a bigger story, the story of the Jewish people during World War II. Understanding my trajectory means to understand the history of Europe, the history of the world back then. How many millions of lives changed during that period? It was on May 10, 1940 that my life changed forever. Hitler invaded Holland with his powerful *Luftwaffe*, the German Air Force, and in a matter of hours they had taken over the most important parts of the country. Holland had been targeted by the Führer due to its proximity to France, one of the biggest enemies of Nazi Germany. Defenseless before the German invasion, the Dutch government surrendered within five days, leaving its people in the hands of the Nazis. It was the beginning of the end.

However, it was all peaceful before Hitler arrived. I was born on April 6, 1929 in Amsterdam, the capital of the Netherlands, to a Dutch father and a South African mother.

Helene, my mother, was a woman ahead of her time and had worked as a secretary before marrying my father. When my maternal grandfather passed away, one of my mother's oldest sisters—there were four in all—studied to become a teacher and started teaching to contribute to the household income, which was being supported by one of their aunts. Soon, she encouraged her younger sisters to study to become secretaries and start working—it was certainly a house full of modern women. My mother got married when she was twenty-five and, even though she became a stay-at-home mom, she continued to be a strong woman. One of her main legacies is the education she gave her children. Her dedication and her teachings certainly gave me a path to follow, even when it became unbearable to live.

I learned about death at an early age and understood how it can change our lives.

I learned about death at an early age and understood how it can change our lives. Willem, my younger brother, was born with a heart condition and died at the age of four. My mother already knew it was bound to happen and had prepared herself for it, as she prepared us as well. I remember this one day, soon after my brother's passing, when she said, "Nanne, my dear, one day they will find a cure. Unfortunately, Willem did not live long enough to see it. When you have a child one day, do not worry about it." My little brother's death, unfortunately, would be my first big loss in life.

My father was as much an admirable person as my mother. Martijn Willem was Dutch and had always been a promising young man. Having a university degree was not the norm in the early twentieth century, so he went to the Amsterdam Business School. Soon he joined the Bank of Amsterdam and, little by little, was promoted to roles of increasing responsibility until he became a director. He was very intelligent and spoke several languages. One day, back from a Scandinavian business trip, he said, "Nanne, next time I go there, I'll be able to speak their language." I never doubted he would.

They were loving parents and always tried to teach my brother and me, in their own way, how to become responsible people. Studying and getting good grades? That was not *their* responsibility. We were the ones who had to know when to do our homework, when to study for a test, and what we needed to do to improve. Thinking back to the happy days we shared, I cannot thank them enough for the way they decided to raise us. Concentration camps were a place where the Nazis wanted to extinguish the Jewish people. For them, there were no families or human beings at those camps. I was not Martijn and Helene's younger daughter; I was just another prisoner without a face, without a name, without any rights. How could I have ever survived at a camp if I still felt the need to be by my parents' side?

Life was normal in elementary school. Segregation had not started yet, which means that Christians and Jews went to class together. We still lived in freedom and I enjoyed it well. Even though I was not often scolded, every time I think about those days I have a smile on my face, because I was far from being a well-behaved child—I must have driven my parents mad sometimes. In my childhood memories, I remember going up on the roof and eating apples from a neighbor's tree. I was a tomboy. My brother, Bernard Martijn, was two years my senior and better behaved. It is hard to believe that, between the two of us, I was the one supposed to be a lady.

We used to live in a large three-story house. I liked doing gymnastics and enjoyed the ample space to practice my routines. Try to imagine my mother calling me for dinner while I was hanging from gymnastics rings... You must make the most out of good and happy times! We never know what will happen next, and never could we have imagined what was about to happen to us.

I also enjoyed reading books, newspapers, everything I could get my hands on! I used to go down to the front door to fetch my father's paper early in the morning and liked reading the headlines as I went back upstairs. How come he never thought it strange that I always took so long to go up those steps? Maybe he did, but he probably liked knowing his daughter was interested in what happened in the world and had an open mind like her mother.

You must make the most out of good, happy times! We never know what will happen next, and never could we have imagined what was about to happen to us.

Now I see that my parents encouraged us to form our own opinion and not have other people's views imposed on us, especially if those views would only prevent the world from evolving. That was how they dealt with religion, for example. We were never traditional, orthodox Jews. My mother actually used to say that she never liked overdoing anything, and my father was a born liberal. Still, that does not mean our education was not molded by religious principles. My father made me study with a young rabbi for five years, since he thought it was important for me to learn our history. We did not go to the synagogue religiously. However, whenever required, my father was perfectly capable of conducting a *minyan*, which is a public prayer that requires a quorum of ten adult Jewish men.

Things changed as the years passed. I remember November 1938, the Night of the Broken Glass, when Jewish properties were looted and synagogues were burned down throughout Germany. Hitler had clearly started to put his plan into action, banishing and exterminating the Jewish people. In Holland, however, people continued not to perceive the imminent danger looming over the country. Since we had remained neutral during World War I, everyone believed the same could happen again.

In addition to that neutrality during World War I, Holland had also become a safe haven due to its veiled antisemitism. Yes, there was antisemitism, but it was not as explicit in Holland as it was in Poland, for example, where Hitler had clearly planted the seed in a fertile ground. When he published "Mein Kampf" in 1925, which he had written during his time in prison, his message about us "parasites" resonated in that setting. Besides that, Germany had been devastated financially, politically, and socially after World War I, and all parties were ready to play their role. I remember my father saying he was "a bank director, despite being Jewish."

I remember my father saying he was "a bank director, despite being Jewish."

After May 10, 1940, there was no doubt in anyone's mind: The situation would only get worse for the Jewish community in Holland. The Nazis soon established that all Dutch people should update their records and state whether they were Jewish. My family and I signed our death sentence on March 22, 1941. Those records, as well as the administration of all ghettos in Poland—where Jews were practically being kept prisoners—were managed by Jewish Councils assembled by the Nazis. Those institutions played a very controversial role during the Holocaust.

With time, Jewish people were at the margin of society, and I watched as my freedom was taken from me. Life for everyone in Holland, including my very own, had taken a turn for the worst. By the end of 1940, public officials who were Jewish had been fired, and so were Jewish teachers. Soon, more measures were taken to isolate us from the Dutch, showing us that we had no right to live in Holland.

We were banned from public transportation, public parks, and movie theaters. Several businesses had put up signs that read "Prohibited for Jews."

I could no longer ride my bike. We were banned from public transportation, public parks and movie theaters. Several businesses had put up signs that read "Prohibited for Jews" much to my distress. Whenever we went to the few places we were still allowed in, we had to wear our yellow badge, the Star of David, which singled us out at all times and made me feel extremely vulnerable. Additionally, Jewish individuals were banned from having a business, or even an occupation. Unfortunately, despite the bank's attempts to keep such an important leader, my father was let go eventually. I still cannot believe how insane this all was. What I did not know was that it would all become even more desperately hard to understand as Hitler's plans moved forward.

After an operation organized with German precision, the Nazis had enough information about Jews in Holland to carry on with their abusive treatment. By the end of 1941, Jewish people were informed that they could no longer choose the school they wanted to go to. Twenty-five Jewish schools were opened in Holland and I had to start going to one of them. I cannot remember what I felt the exact moment I heard the news. It was simply something we needed to do, and so we did it. But try to imagine a twelve-year-old girl who was curious about the world, who was starting to learn things about herself and had to change her entire concept of life in such an abrupt way. I was banned from seeing my Christian classmates; I could not go to their houses or celebrate their birthdays. We just had to accept it, as if the Germans had become gods guiding our lives, playing with our destiny. Motivated by fear, most Dutch people accepted those decisions without questioning or protesting them. There was not a thing we could do and that was how we were supposed to go on with our lives.

It was at the new Jewish school that I met a beautiful scrawny girl who had a captivating smile and caught everyone's attention with her stories and intelligent talk. By a mere coincidence, Anne Frank and I went to the same school and were in the same classroom. We were all Jewish there, teachers and students, which made it all more dramatic during the war. In our first year, there were thirty students in my class; by the second year, there were only sixteen of us. People simply started disappearing and were never heard from again—nobody talked about them either. Were they hiding, or had they been deported? By the end of July 1942, the Dutch press announced that the Nazis had decided to send Jews to labor camps in Germany.

By a mere coincidence, Anne Frank and I went to the same school and were in the same classroom.

Since deportation was the most devastating scenario, we lived in constant fear that each one of us and our close relatives would be taken away. You would wake up one day and your cousins were gone; the next day, your grandmother had been deported and disappeared as if she had never existed. These were traumatic times. And it was in that environment of collective suffering and concern that we were able to stay united at school. We were aware that those were tough times of fear and oppression, and that is why we did not want to make matters worse or cause a rift. The harmony the world was lacking then was being fully experienced by a group of Jewish kids who were not older than fourteen.

During the time Anne and I spent at the Jewish school, I was able to attend a party for her thirteenth birthday.

Anne Frank disappeared one day, too. She and her family went into hiding in early July 1942 and started to live in a secret annex located at her father's company Opekta Werke, which made ingredients for fruit jam. The word out in the street was that they had run away, but nobody knew for sure.

However, during the time Anne and I spent at the Jewish school, I was able to attend a party for her thirteenth birthday. I remember watching some sort of advertising about jam manufacturing before a Rin Tin Tin movie—back then, films were stored in cans. There was a war outside, so we only had a very modest snack, and our curfew was at eight at night. Some biographers have wrongly written that I gave her a bookmark, but the truth is that I gave her a brooch—I remember as if it were today. I also witnessed the moment she received her beloved diary, which later became so famous. No one in the Franks' living room could have ever imagined that those bound sheets of paper would one day contain words capable of moving readers worldwide. There was so much that none of us in that room could have ever imagined. Anne dreamed of becoming a writer, but none of what later became a reality had ever been in our dreams—those were things our worst nightmares were made of.

I also witnessed the moment she received her beloved diary, which later became so famous.

By late September 1943, we were sleeping one day when our slumber was interrupted early in the morning by the cruel reality. Someone was knocking on our door, as if they were trying to knock it down. I cannot remember whether my mother or my father answered the door. All I know is that I could hear my own heartbeat, which was getting louder and louder with each passing moment, and that I was afraid someone could hear it too and be irritated by it. Suddenly, the four of us were standing there before the Nazis. We did not know what to do while they verbally abused us and rushed us out of the door, out of our own home, with the few clothes and belongings we were able to grab. As it was the case, Pulse, a moving company hired by the Nazis to empty the homes of deported Jews, later came and took over our house and everything valuable inside. To this day, I still cannot understand how Hitler got away with it. He transformed men and women into brutal animals without any sense of humanity. That is only one of the many things I still wonder about. After September 1943, while the Nazis were hunting the last Jews in hiding, Holland was declared a Jewish-free country.

2

UNCERTAIN FUTURE

Hitler would always play with us. After using the organization and structure created with the aid of the Jewish Council and banning Jews from using public transportation, he put me and my family inside a street car and sent us to our uncertain future—our uncertain and hopeless future. What else could I feel then besides fear? There is no other feeling I remember experiencing so deeply during that time. Fear had become my best friend.

My father had never considered the possibility of our family going into hiding, as other Dutch Jews had done at the first sign of imminent danger. In order to find a hiding place, you needed money and had to trust those who would help you hide—and there was always the possibility of being betrayed and deported. Besides, the end of the war was a mystery to everyone. How long would we have to stay hidden? Still, I know he trusted the word and good faith of a female lawyer, and thought it was enough to feel safe.

What happened was that my mother's birth certificate was issued in South Africa (she no longer had a copy of it by then) and it did not state her religion. Since it did not identify her as Jewish, the female lawyer said she could get a document that would help us. That came with a price, of course. She never gave us that document and betrayed us instead, as she had done with so many other families.

Those who went into hiding were not safe, since they were afraid they would be found out and that someone would report them in exchange of a reasonable sum of money.

It is amazing how war can bring the best and worst out of people. The events we experienced and witnessed showed us most of people's worst side, unfortunately. Those who went into hiding were not safe, since they were afraid they would be found out and that someone would report them in exchange of a reasonable sum of money. What can I say? Those were times of war.

After we were captured, we were taken through deserted streets to a train station in Amstel. How come no one tried to help us? How come no one did anything? As a matter of fact, everyone was terrified of doing anything at all. Helping a Jew was a death sentence back then. Nobody came to our aid, and that is why we were there, ready to leave.

A train station can lead to many destinations: holidays, business trips, visits to distant relatives. That train station, however, would take us to a terrible fate against our will. Our destination was Westerbork, a transitional camp in the Drenthe province, northeast Holland. Ours is a small country, so the trip would be short, only a few hours long. I remember some guards were with us on the train. They wanted to make sure we would not escape and indeed reach our destination, as if we were the worst criminals in the world.

The Westerbork camp had been built by the Dutch government in 1939 to welcome Jewish people who had run away from Germany and were in constant fear of what the Nazi Party meant for their safety. It became a very useful building to the Germans' perverse interests. By late 1941, the Germans had decided that Westerbork was the ideal place for a transitional camp to host Dutch Jews before they were deported to extermination camps. In July 1942, Germans had taken control of the place and their operation was put in place; one quick stop in Westerbork before being sent to die.

The train went right into the camp. Westerbork was a totally inhospitable place with a dull, gray landscape, far removed from anything that reminded me of the city we had left, where both my early life and most recent existence had involved playing and enjoying complete freedom. However, when I look back at that time, I think about the days that came after my brief stay in Westerbork, and I now know that it was a better place to live in a time of war.

The camp had a main path with barracks on both sides. I looked around and saw some guards and watchtowers. It was the somber, solitary backdrop of a prison. Who was paying for all that? Literally, we were, because camp maintenance and expansion were being financed with properties confiscated from the Jewish people.

We arrived with our belongings and they took us to a registration desk. We were supposed to state our name and where we were coming from, even though we did not know what we were doing there. This process was repeated in all concentration camps managed by the Nazis for everyone who was not selected to go to the gas chamber upon their arrival—if they had arrived at an extermination camp, that is. Ironically, after the war was over, that was the exact same process that allowed surviving relatives to trace back the last steps of many victims.

When we were going through the registration process, my family and I could hardly speak. My brother, who already was a discrete person, was extremely frightened. We all had a concerned look on our face.

Fugitives were considered "condemned Jews" and had to wear blue overalls and wooden clogs. They also had

to remain in a punishment block, were forced to work under the worst of conditions, and their food rations were smaller.

We were allowed to keep our own clothes, unlike those who had been in hiding prior to deportation, as it was the case with Anne Frank and her family after they were found in their hiding place in August 1944. Fugitives were considered "condemned Jews" and had to wear blue overalls and wooden clogs. They also had to remain in a punishment block, were forced to work under the worst of conditions, and their food rations were smaller. Anne's family had to work disassembling old batteries. What was the purpose of their work? We did not know, as we did not know the purpose of many jobs assigned to Jewish people who had been sent to concentration camps.

After the registration process, we were sent to our barracks. My mother and I had to go to the women's barrack, while my father and my brother were sent to the men's barrack. Even though we slept in separate areas, we had a little bit of freedom during the day to spend time together, which was something we did as often as we could. We slept in bunk beds, a luxury compared to the conditions we would be subjected to later on, or the situation encountered by those who had been able to survive gas chambers in Auschwitz.

Westerbork seemed like a paradoxical place to me, since it hosted thousands of refugees from different places. It was a transitional camp, so it received sporadic visitors and, at the same time, it housed people who had created a community and found a home there. There were schools, a theater, and hospitals, for example, among other structures where German Jews participated intensely, since they had been there from the very beginning.

Dutch Jews who were to be deported did not remain there for more than a few days, maybe weeks. We met people we knew from Amsterdam, but we would lose touch with them quickly, since they would soon board a train to the worst of their nightmares. My family and I remained there for a longer period of time, which gave us hope and, at the same time, made us anxious day after day—and I remember those days being endless sometimes.

Due to my father's respected position, our names were put on the Palestine list that, among other purposes, included Jewish people who could be exchanged for German individuals who had been made prisoners of war. That meant we could have a little bit of hope that one day we would be far away from that place, away from that situation. That hope was ultimately just an illusion.

We had to stand in long lines to heat our food in space heaters and we took cold showers, even during winter. Instead of restrooms, we had latrines.

We had a reasonable amount of food, enough not to go hungry. However, we had lost the comfort of our home. We had to stand in long lines to heat our food in space heaters and we took cold showers, even during winter. Instead of restrooms, we had latrines. Arriving at that place and going through that situation was something that changed my concept of hygiene. We unfortunately could not do anything about it but feel very uncomfortable.

I did not work at Westerbork, but often helped look after the children, who one day would leave alongside adults to their fateful end. At least children could entertain themselves there sometimes. We used to sing and play with them, adding a little bit of fantasy to such a colorless environment. Adults did what they could to protect children from that situation.

My brother and I, who were sixteen and fourteen years old respectively, were no longer children. Besides, the situation had made us mature more quickly than it would have been natural to kids our age, and we did everything possible not to make our parents worry about us. Eventually, we heard conversations about what was happening, but we were not aware of it all. During our time in this transitional camp, I remember my father went to Amsterdam a few times. What could he possibly have done there? I do not know, and his trips remain a mystery to me to this day.

Westerbork was a relatively quiet place. However, it was all an illusion for Jewish people to cooperate with that repugnant plan and believe everything would be alright. Unlike concentration camps, there were very few Nazis around and they were only responsible for guarding the perimeter, while the Dutch police was in charge of keeping the order inside. I believe the Nazis were there only to make sure deported individuals would indeed leave for their destination. Since some Jewish people were only there for very few days, I imagine they were unable to capture what "life" was like in that place.

Apart from this seemingly worry-free life, anxiety was a constant in our daily routine. Every Monday, names were read out loud to inform those who had to present themselves for deportation. It was something horrible! Those on the list were terribly desperate upon hearing their names, while those who were not called always sighed in relief. We never knew where we would be taken, but knowing was always better than imagining the unknown, since we were already aware of the existence of extermination camps. Our relief did not last more than a week, though, since names would be read again the following Monday and we would hope with all our strength our family name was not called. Those being taken to extermination camps would have to be at the internal yard and ready to leave on a train the next day. Now, looking back, I cannot imagine anything more grotesque than this scenario: Families gathering the few belongings they had been able to keep, just to be sent to their deaths. What kind of humanity is this?

Anne Frank went through the same routine: She heard her name being read from a list and was assigned to a train that left September 3rd, 1944 to Auschwitz.

Anne Frank went through the same routine: She heard her name being read from a list and was assigned to a train that left September 3rd, 1944 to Auschwitz. It was one of the last means of transportation in Holland that still left to one of the most feared camps, and the entire Frank family joined four other people with whom they had shared their hiding place.

Operations in the Westerbork camp were organized from a distance by Albert Gemmeker, the German camp commander and a character that remains mysterious to this day. He used to promote cultural manifestations inside the camp and was never seen punishing any prisoners—which was something that German guards seemed to take pleasure in doing. Every Tuesday he was there, placid and alert, watching what could have been the opening scenes of a horror movie.

Due to poor hygiene conditions, my mother got lice. Camps were infested with lice and it was extremely unnerving to have to live with those disgusting insects, unable to do anything about them, without medicine or any chance of staying clean. That event caused my mother to have a nervous breakdown.

When I think about those long days we spent waiting for something to happen, I still do not understand how I was able to look ahead. The future was a big question mark. What I knew for sure was that they had taken me away from school, away from my life, and brutally dragged me out of my house, and now I was waiting for a future that did not show a single sign of optimism. How could I react to that? How could I overcome those endless days? What hope could I have for my life from there on out?

Tension and anxiety were so overwhelming that, one day, all of a sudden, I fainted in the middle of the camp.

Tension and anxiety were so overwhelming that, one day, all of a sudden, I fainted in the middle of the camp. I suddenly lost consciousness and an older lady came to my aid. I came to as she gently patted my face so that I could wake up. I perhaps fainted due to the precarious conditions we were subjected to, but most certainly due to my constantly frayed nerves. Had my body tried to help me escape what seemed like a nightmare?

And that is how we lived our life in Westerbork: Keeping our family united under those circumstances and trying to keep our constantly haunting thoughts at bay. Endless months went by until the winter of 1944, and what made it all even more distressing was the fact that we did not have any hot water or anything else that could bring us some comfort against the cold. Would it have been better for us to stay there until the end of the war? At least we would be able to survive there. However, the Germans were not planning for our survival.

The Germans were not planning for our survival.

On February 14, 1944 we were once again waiting to hear the names of people who would leave and go to an unknown place. This time, my family would not experience that familiar momentary relief: Martijn Willem, Helene, Nanette and Bernard had to present ourselves the following day to leave on the next train towards deportation. That routine had been repeated many times in our absence, and its final day would be September 15, 1944, when the last train left Westerbork to the Bergen-Belsen camp taking a few people and leaving at least one thousand prisoners at the transitional camp.

While some would leave quickly, my family and I remained there for four months. I could not tell whether leaving would be the end or only the beginning. The same scene that I had witnessed so many times now had my own family as protagonists. The four of us were tense and anxious as we waited for the train. Intimately, I hoped that train would never come, so we would never have to leave. That did not happen, though, and we had to board the train.

What we felt at that crucial moment? A little bit of relief, because we knew we would be going to Bergen-Belsen, a camp that was known for its better conditions compared to the rest of them. Still, that relief would be brief—there would be no worry-free moments after that day.

3

FIRST IMPRESSIONS OF BERGEN-BELSEN

We did not know what to expect from Bergen-Belsen. We were able to spend months in Westerbork without apparently being at risk of dying. Would we be that "lucky" in Bergen-Belsen? We were bound to yet another completely unknown place controlled by the Nazis, which was certainly not a good environment for Jewish people.

Once again we were on board of a regular train. Later we found out that it had been a "privilege" we were entitled to, since deported Jews destined for extermination camps would leave in cattle wagons fitted with a bucket latrine and without any food to eat—those were really inhumane conditions. Besides, trains going westbound had to cover longer distances and took days until they would reach their final destination.

The train transporting us was immersed in a silence that screamed louder than words. Everyone was afraid of talking about our predicament. When someone spoke, it was brief. I remember that, since the German occupation, my mother used to ask my brother and me to be careful about what we said because "the walls have ears."

Germany, the feared enemy territory, was our destination. Along our trip, we were not given any food. SS soldiers, wearing black uniform, heavy military boots, and a hat, kept us company. There was something sinister about them, as if their faces never relaxed and the somber look in their eyes never changed. They also wore a belt with the inscription *Gott ist mit uns*, "God is with us." What kind of god would that be? It could only be a malignant god like Hitler, who made all possible efforts to teach his followers to serve him.

The SS, or *Schutzstaffel*, was created in 1925 and its purpose was to become an elite squad that would protect Adolf Hitler. What did it take to become part of such an elite squad? Of course Hitler would not take anyone with minimum "qualifications." Well, in order to be responsible for the safety of the Nazi leader, one had to be a member of the Aryan race and passionately loyal to the Nazi Party. It comes as no surprise that the SS motto was *Mein Ehre heisst Treue*, "My honor is loyalty." Clearly, Hitler was not looking for regular workers but followers of his doctrine who would be able to make his system work.

Starting in 1929, the SS was under Heinrich Himmler's command, and he was just as perverse as Hitler, the leader. Himmler was one of the most important men in the Nazi Party, at the same level as Hermann Göring (Aviation Minister), Joseph Goebbels (Propaganda Minister), and Martin Bormann (the Führer's personal secretary). At first, the elite squad was small, but it soon grew under Himmler's command to absorb other organizations within the Nazi Party. That was how the SS, or Himmler, started to control concentration camps in 1939, then extermination camps in 1941. It is estimated that throughout World War II, the SS had about one million members. Obviously, Hitler would have not been able to implement his perverse plan all by himself.

It is estimated that throughout World War II, the SS had about one million members. Obviously, Hitler would

have not been able to implement his perverse plan all by himself.

During our train ride to Germany, we could not imagine what kind of guards would accompany us, or what they would be capable of doing. For a fourteen-year-old girl, however, their serious posture and somber look were enough to make me terrified. Those Nazis certainly were not there to make friends with us.

Similarly to Holland, the German countryside has a very bucolic landscape during summer. It was winter, and the gray tones that surrounded us were highlighted by the disquiet in our souls. As the train followed the tracks, images were flashing before my eyes: the holidays we spent in Switzerland, our trips to meet relatives in England, the games my brother and I would play. Would we ever have happy moments again? Would we ever go back to a normal life in our house? Could I, in the future, grow up, study, have an occupation? There was no way of knowing.

I felt a pit in my stomach upon reaching German territory.

I felt a pit in my stomach upon reaching German territory. That was where it all had begun. That was where, in 1933, German citizens had democratically elected a leader who preached that the country should get rid of everything impure—including the Jews. What could they do to us there? People with such beautiful, serene features, with apparently sweet children who were smiling and playing... How could they do anything bad to us?

When the train arrived at its final destination, my heart started to beat faster. It is one thing to imagine what could happen, but when your imagination becomes a reality, there is nothing left to do but move forward. Could we have attempted to run away from that train? Would the SS guards mistakenly give us an opportunity to escape somewhere far away? In order to prevent prisoners from escaping, though, there were members of the SS on top of the train as well. There were times when passengers became desperate and tried to escape after looking through the small gaps in cattle wagons and seeing Poland, only to realize that they were bound to Auschwitz-Birkenau. Escapees would have a limb amputated or be killed. The chances of successfully escaping were practically non-existent.

Unlike what had happened in Westerbork, our stop was not a camp. Where would we go from there? What could we expect? Everyone got up from their seats and gathered the few belongings they were able to take with them. We walked towards the exit as if in a trance since we had no other option. What would they have done if I rebelled against them and refused to get off the train? What if I refused to move for a second and threw a tantrum, as is typical of teenagers? I believe I certainly would not be here now. There was no room for disobedience in Nazi Germany.

There was no room for disobedience in Nazi Germany.

When we stepped out of the train it was as if I had been electrocuted. Reality presented itself before my eyes. Several SS men were calmly organized in a line, as if going about a regular day at work, next to their huge, ferocious German shepherds. Those dogs were the face of terror itself. They barked and stared at us with a demonic look in their eyes, longing for a bite. I hoped with all my heart they could not free themselves and get any closer to my family and me.

From that moment on we understood the role the SS guards had been playing. They were certainly not there to help us—they had been trained to humiliate and torment us for as long as they could. That was the first shocking comparison to Westerbork, since there were only a few Nazis there, and they almost never bothered us. However, Germans were in charge of concentration camps, not the Dutch police or German-Jewish people. My fear and tension were only intensified after that moment.

The SS men approached with their dogs, yelling at us in German. They were swearing while telling us to walk in a line, since we would have a long way to go until Bergen-Belsen. We quickly stood in a line and waited for them to lead us in the right direction. From that moment on nobody dared to protest and we looked down fearing for any eye contact we could have with one another.

This was a defining moment. We had been taken away from our house, spent months in Westerbork without knowing what the future would hold for us—which was already cause for much concern—but we had survived and been safe so far. Now, the true reality revealed itself before us. I was walking in that line, with those beasts that had been trained to hurt anyone who did not follow orders, side by side with men who did not show any indication they would ever do anything to help us. Undoubtedly, there was no room for illusion any longer.

We were in northern Germany, near Hanover and Celle—the latter was a medieval city with castles and an air of a small town. Nothing we were living through held any resemblance to the lives of Germans residents who were so close to us.

Were those German residents in their homes, eating a warm meal comfortably? Did they have the opportunity to stay home without being bothered? They certainly did. At that time, we were already aware that we had no right to lead a normal life, and the word "comfort" would be forever scratched from our dictionary in that concentration camp. From the moment we lost our house there was no hope for us.

We walked through a wintery landscape with many leafless trees and the noise of the wind. The cold winter was about to bid us farewell and make way for spring. The scenery was certainly beautiful—so beautiful bad things should not be allowed to take place there. Why

25

did they take place at all then? The German guards and their dogs were the only ones allowed to make a sound; we had no permission to say anything, to ask where we were going or what they intended to do with us. We did not even have the right to protest and complain about that we did not wish to be there.

The situation was such that our parents were afraid for their own lives, like helpless children, unable to do anything about it.

My parents were nearby and also looked extremely apprehensive. Children see their parents as a safe haven, the assurance that everything will be okay. If something is wrong, children know where to run, whose shoulder to cry on. However, the situation was such that our parents were afraid for their own lives, like helpless children, unable to do anything about it. Facing that predicament, I could not hold them responsible for whatever happened to me. From that moment on I would have to take care of myself. I had no idea what that would entail though, and what level of independence would be demanded of me.

We had been walking for over half an hour, and it did not seem to matter that we had not had anything to eat since we left Westerbork. Sometimes we, human beings, tend to believe we have no strength left to endure certain events that are imposed on us. When that happens, there is nothing else we can do but move forward. Obviously, there are certain situations in which the unbearable becomes insurmountable—and that was something I would only learn in Bergen-Belsen.

We finally reached the camp, after having taken so many anxious steps along the way. I paid attention to the shuffling noise we had been making. I also took notice of the railroads. Since the intense commotion in Westerbork on Tuesdays, when prisoners were supposedly leaving for work camps, I could no longer see railroads as something positive. Today I know my suspicions were correct. Those railroads represented the crumbling of the Jewish community.

At first sight, Bergen-Belsen seemed like a bad place. The landscape was not very nice to look at—or to live in for that matter. It was a large property with several barracks surrounded by barbed wire. It was a horrible view. Why would they need all that? Was it meant to protect or to hurt people in Bergen-Belsen? It certainly could not be something good.

That place was made up by several camps separated from one another by barbed wire. It was a really big property, and I wondered where we would be placed. As we got closer, the impression I got was that we were not about to spend pleasant days there and our life would not be easy. As I looked at the watchtowers and the SS soldiers holding their guns, I could not see ourselves ever leaving that place. I asked myself if, one day, I would have a normal house again, in a setting that would not make me feel like one of the worst people in the world, as if we had committed a crime for simply being alive. I am sure all Jewish families did not know what was waiting for them and did not expect much from the future.

I cannot tell whether I had already realized what being in a concentration camp would mean to me, to my life. You can only understand a place like that when you live in it—there is no other way of knowing any better. Still, you cannot fully grasp it because you cannot comprehend that which exists cannot be comprehended.

Back then, most of our acquaintances, relatives and friends were going through the same situation, the same routine in camps—that is, if they were not dead already. Dutch deportations started in July 1942, and Holland was only one of the countries where that operation was taking place.

When the plan was first implemented, Nazi Germany acted carefully and used euphemisms to mask their intentions, stating that the Jews would be taken to work camps, and people apparently did not know what it meant. With time, other measures were adopted, and it became clearer what the Germans wished to accomplish, or the level of cruelty their plan would bring about.

Upon rising to power, Hitler dealt with the "Jewish problem" in practical terms, and only within German territory. Jews had to leave his country, as it was the case with the Frank family, which fled from Frankfurt to Holland in 1933, where they would supposedly be safer. A few months later, however, the idea of confining those who opposed the regime—or had been considered opposers—finally took shape. The Dachau camp was then built in a former gun powder factory in the outskirts of Dachau, Germany. Gypsies, homosexuals, and Jews were taken there. As the war escalated and European countries were invaded—several of them were occupied by Nazi Germany—the Nazis started to deal with the "Jewish problem" at a continental scale.

The issue became critical in Eastern European countries, such as Poland and the Soviet Union, where antisemitism was intense. Hitler had signed the Molotov-Ribbentrop pact, a nonaggression treaty with the Soviet Union, which was later ratified in 1939. Nevertheless, in order to fulfil Nazi ambitions, the pact was ignored in June 1941, when German troops invaded Soviet territory, which was then under Josef Stalin's command. After the invasion, Himmler was in charge of safeguarding the occupied country and had authority to physically eliminate anyone who got in the way of their plans—a reality that became very dramatic.

Initially, prisoners were killed by inhaling carbon monoxide generated by diesel engines. As the Nazi wished for a more efficient extermination process, they turned to Zyklon B.

Extermination camps with gas chambers were first established in Poland. Initially, prisoners were killed by inhaling carbon monoxide generated by diesel engines. As the Nazis wished for a more efficient extermination process, they turned to Zyklon B, a fabric disinfectant, and used it in pill form, which made the chemical become lethal when in contact with the air. That solution was used to kill thousands of prisoners at once in camps like Majdanek, Treblinka, and Auschwitz-Birkenau. Nazi leaders gathered in the Wannsee Conference held on January 20, 1942 to discuss the "Final Solution," whose objective was to exterminate the Jewish people. Upon our arrival at Bergen-Belsen, one of the many Nazi concentration camps, we were unaware of the dimensions of such plan.

When we arrived at Bergen-Belsen, my grandmother and a few cousins had already been deported to Sobibor, an extermination camp in Poland, where some prisoners had attempted to break free—that was the one and only attempt of that kind. Prisoners plotted to kill all guards and run away. On October 14, 1943, when the plan was to be put into action, the operation was unveiled after a few SS military guards were killed. Only a small group of prisoners was able to escape, while others were captured and killed. Those who did not attempt to flee and remained in the camp were also killed by the SS. After all, if one of them survived, they could tell the world the horrible things they had been put through. Today, after looking through the records, we know that my dear grandmother Marie was deported to Sobibor on April 23, 1943, where she passed away.

During the war though, we had no way of knowing what happened to those who were deported to other camps. The lack of information made us feel terrible. People disappeared, people we loved, people we saw every day, and there was nothing we could do about it. We started to imagine what could have happened, but there were no trails to follow. We were going through the same thing, and our own future was uncertain as well. What would happen to *us*?

It may sound odd to the young generation that we did not know what was going on at the time. We must keep in mind that times were different back then, and means of communication did not work like they do now. Concentration camps, especially extermination camps, were placed in remote, inhospitable locations. Besides, when someone shows up at your home holding a gun, when the law and so many people are against you, there is not much you can do, and you cannot show resistance to them. The Nazis did not want to leave any trace and let others put an end to their plan.

It is incredible how your fear can escalate when you see the people you love feeling as helpless as you do. When we entered Bergen-Belsen, I felt a sense of terror in my chest upon realizing that I would have to fight for my life and, at the same time, be constantly worried about the safety of my father, mother, and brother. We had to stay together, go on together, and remain safe until we could see a change in our situation. God, when would that horrible war spreading throughout a devastated Europe ever end?

The Bergen-Belsen camp was created in 1940 and, at first, it was exclusively reserved for prisoners of war. In April 1943, Himmler's SS took control to turn it into a residential camp and, later, a concentration camp.

These camps were divided into sub camps that worked in different periods. Residence camps were in operation until April 1945, and they were divided into four smaller camps: Special Camp (*Sonderlager*), Neutral Camp (*Neutralenlager*), Star Camp (*Sternlager*) and Hungarian Camp (*Ungarnlager*). At the Special Camp, there were Jewish people with immigration passports from other countries, especially South America. Most people sent there did not survive, and many were sent to Auschwitz-Birkenau to be exterminated in gas chambers. The Neutral Camp received European Jews from countries that had remained neutral during the war, as it was the case with Spain and Turkey. Conditions at those camps were considered good, and it is said that prisoners in that area were not treated with so much cruelty.

The Star Camp was bigger than the others, and Jewish people from the Palestine list were sent there—in theory, they lived in better conditions. Germans considered Jews in that camp as "merchandise," and they needed to maintain proper appearance in order to be offered in exchange for something. Besides, Germany wanted to keep the Red Cross away from these camps in order to do whatever they pleased and prevent retaliation from other countries or any damage to their image worldwide. Lastly, the Hungarian Camp received Hungarian Jews that Himmler also planned to offer in exchange for money or goods.

Prisoner camps consisted of the original prisoner camp, as well as the Convalescence Camp (*Erholungslager*), the Small Women's Camp (*Kleines Frauenlager*), the Tent Camp (*Zeltlager*) and the Large Women's Camp (*Grosses Frauenlager*).

These structures were not connected, and prisoners could not move freely from one camp to another. Consequently, even if you knew someone who had been sent to the same camp, you might never get to see each other there. After the war, I was in touch with several acquaintances who had also been to Bergen-Belsen, but we were unaware of it back then. Honestly, that place was like a large prison.

If a place has a crematorium, people are not expected to stay alive there for a long time.

We were not in an extermination camp, but I noticed there was a crematorium there. And, if a place has a crematorium, people are not expected to stay alive there for a long time.

We took a cold shower after entering the camp. I had never been more embarrassed my entire life, and we all had to take off our clothes and shower in front of other people, no matter how much that bothered us and made us feel violated. Hot water, good soap, a towel to dry off? These were luxury items we did not have the right to use. Considering the way we were being treated and the names they were calling us, it was clear from the moment we arrived that we, Jews, had no dignity there. Your story, who you were, and what you had accomplished so far did not mean anything there; we were nothing but repulsive parasites.

After showering, we were sent to the registration desk. One of the first things that got my attention in Bergen-Belsen was the fact that there were no birds flying and chirping. It was intriguing, since we were in an area with many trees and green fields during summer, but yet there was no sign of life around us. Well, what bird would draw inspiration from barbed wires, watchtowers, guns, and frightened faces? There surely would not be any beautiful songs from free birds. Nature was manifesting itself, its opinion and consternation for what was taking place in Bergen-Belsen, for what was happening during those terrible times.

At the registration desk, we had to state our name and where we were coming from. Did they really care that my name was Nanette Blitz, that I was born in Holland, and that I really liked doing gymnastics? Did they care that my father was an intelligent man and, so far, had had a promising career in business? No, they did not care about that at all. We were just another number in that immense operation.

Since we were in the Palestine list, we were sent to the Star Camp, named after the yellow Star of David that indicated we were Jewish. Besides, we were allowed to keep our own clothes and did not have to have our heads shaven or numbers tattooed on our skin. We were considered privileged and there was a possibility that we could be exchanged for something and go somewhere far from Bergen-Belsen. However, that possibility became an illusion because very few prisoners were effectively freed under those conditions.

Everyone who went to other camps was not allowed to keep their clothes and had to wear something that resembled striped pajamas. Can you imagine what it was like to wear the same clothes every day, without any other option? With time, the situation would become really repulsive. Even though I never wore that uniform, that is probably the reason why I do not wear stripes to this day. This is only one of the infamous memories I would catalog in my mind throughout my life after being sent to a concentration camp.

As I mentioned before, unlike Westerbork, which managed by German-Jews, Bergen-Belsen was operated by Himmler's SS—and he was known to be cold and cruel. There, we would not have a commander like Gemmeker, who watched plays acted by Jewish people in Westerbork. From the moment we stepped off the train, during that long walk, and while we had our information recorded, everything seemed to follow a method, even the way we were being disrespected. It became clear to us that nothing there was improvised. It was a well-oiled machine and all pieces had a role to play. We were in touch with true robots who blindly followed Hitler's strategy and doctrine.

After shower and registration, we were sent to our camp and assigned a barrack. My mother and I went to a barrack, while my father and my brother went to another. Again, men and women had to sleep separately. I really wished we were able to stay together, so I could feel safer. Not having my father and my brother with me meant that I would worry about them every time we had to be apart.

I soon noticed our barrack was bigger than the one we had in Westerbork, but there were more women there, too. It was a large space and there were several bunk beds arranged side by side. Once again, there would be no privacy. In our old house, I had a room all to myself, with a warm, clean, comfortable bed. What I and everyone living in that place had was hard wooden bunk beds lined with straw. All that straw had been probably inspired by stables, and that was the best we deserved.

What I and everyone living in that place had was hard wooden bunk beds lined with straw.

Most people at our housing and in the Star Camp were from Holland. There were people of other nationalities, too, including Tunisians, Yugoslavians, and French, but they were in smaller numbers. Concentration camps were like a Tower of Babel: Polish, Czech, Hungarian, and German were some of the languages spoken there. Some people could not understand each other, while others could understand very little, but enough. All that mattered was that we all understood Nazi Germans. Communication was easier in our barrack due to the amount of Dutch spoken there. However, I was able to speak other languages, such as English—my mother had been educated in England and had family there—German, and a little bit of French I had learned at school.

It was depressing to look at that gray, miserable place and imagine that we would stay there for an unknown amount of time, without being certain of what would happen to us. We could not call it a home, and it was odd to say Bergen-Belsen was our home, because it did not have the appearance of a home. It was unmistakably a concentration camp and it had not been built to make prisoners feel comfortable and at ease.

People sent there were also able to keep their belongings in the housing. Along the inside wall of those barracks, there were backpacks containing everything we had been able to carry with us. It was an odd image to me: even though it looked like anyone could just grab their packed things and leave at any moment, I had to remind myself that it would not be possible, because we were being kept in that place, stuck in that situation. I had to remain where I was with the little things I still had.

I slept in a bunk bed near my mother. After the months we spent in Westerbork, that situation did not seem new to me any longer. We had slept in bunk beds there, too, and shared our lives with people we did not know. My father and brother had been sent to a separate barrack there as well, but I had grown used to life in Westerbork, where not so many restrictions were imposed on us. Of course we had been away from home, from the rest of our family, from our life, but Westerbork did not restrict us from surviving, nor did it test our limits as it would happen in our new dwelling.

Despite the anxiety, I fell fast asleep from exhaustion after the trip. Being in that barrack in Bergen-Belsen was the beginning of a new life for me. Everything I knew about life itself, about the life I thought was my own, no longer existed. There was now only constant anxiety and uncertainty about the future. When you find yourself in a concentration camp, your main concern is to survive the present day. We did not think in terms of years anymore; we were only worried about what today would bring us.

What could such a young girl, like I was back then, ever expect from the future? Going to school, learning, growing, making friends, getting ready for adult life, getting married, having a family... The main concerns a young woman should have are getting good grades at school and being a good daughter to her parents. I could only ache for what Bergen-Belsen had prepared for us, and that was what we were about to find out.

4

DAILY LIFE IN THE CAMP

Life in a concentration camp is beyond comprehension. Only those who have gone through it can precisely assess the horror, uncertainty, and abnormality of it all. Oftentimes, even those who have gone through it cannot quite express themselves while sharing their experience, because they have done everything in their power to erase from their memory any trace of what they went through. Having committed no crime at all, one day my family and I were shut off from the world and isolated from society. That fate is only conceived for those who can no longer be part of a community. What crime had we committed in order to end up there? Being Jewish had become a crime, and we were going to pay the price.

We always had a normal, healthy middle-class life in Holland. My father had secured a good job, my mother was a great person and educator and, motivated by our parents, my brother and I were studying to become good people too. However, everything that was ordinary about our lives was taken away from us without any plausible justification or hope for when things would be restored, for when we would go back to normal.

In our past routine, we would wake up, wash our faces, have breakfast and go on with our to-do list for the day. In concentration camps, there were no breakfast tables, towels to dry our faces or toothbrushes. Under normal circumstances we sometimes take these little things for granted, and how good they make us feel. In turn, when these things are taken away, the shock is frightening—you lose your sense of reality. When other survivors and I think back on those days in the camp, it is hard to put it all into words. "Horrifying" is the only definition that comes to mind.

Going through a concentration camp causes a shift in your values.

Going through a place like this causes a shift in your values: you are not the same you were before. We take so many things for granted in life, we do not pay attention to them, and do not know how important they are until they are gone. When that happens, you feel empty, as if nothing makes sense anymore. You feel lost because everything that makes you safe is suddenly gone.

And if life in a concentration camp held no resemblance to a normal life, how could I ever attempt to describe it? Would there be anything similar to a regular routine in a place like that? Our routine now was fighting for survival—that is what we had to do every day: fight every second in order to survive. This kind of behavior demanded discipline every step of the way, so you would not "make a wrong move" and it brought constant fear and anxiety. The relatively calm period in Westerbork was behind us and Bergen-Belsen would be a daily struggle for our life. We knew that as soon as we set foot there.

It was there that the Nazis showed their most cruel face, revealing who they truly were and what perverse goals they had. The routine in that place was set by the mood of those soldiers, who were there to make our lives as unbearable as possible. Every day, there would be a headcount (*Appel*). What was the purpose of those constant, endless headcounts? We had no idea and there were many other things we did not understand about the time we spent there.

In each barrack there was a person in charge of making sure we were all present for the headcount. There was no disputing it—everyone had to participate in that activity. So we would go to this kind of main square, line up and wait for that nightmare to come to an end.

Prisoners had to take part in the headcount even if they were in no condition to do so. You could be sick, unable to move properly—it did not matter: you were either there, or you died. Nazis did not care about the weather, either. They would do a headcount under the pouring rain or during the unbearable winter. Why would they care about how cold it was? They were warm and protected under that uniform; only prisoners had to worry about the cold.

The headcount could take endless hours—it was overwhelming. They would count every prisoner in the camp and, if they lost count for some reason, they would start all over again. I remember this time, when it was so cold one of the prisoners got a frost bite. There was no going around it and they had to amputate his toes. Can you imagine losing your toes because of something that did not even make any sense? That is what life was like for us every day there.

In my memories, I can remember endless hours of waiting, being unable to move during a headcount. On top of subjecting us to that, the Nazis would also bring their vicious dogs to that depressing spectacle. Those dogs were trained to kill. The soldiers in charge of them had thick padding around their forearms to protect themselves in case of an attack. You can imagine what happened when someone without the least protection was bitten by one of those dogs.

Those dogs were trained to kill. The soldiers in charge of them had thick padding around their forearms to protect themselves in case of an attack.

I sometimes wonder if they did it all just to mess with our mental stability and make us even more terrified than we already were. The level of cruelty in those human beings was impressive. They did not have compassion for anything, no matter how bad it was. Were they doing a headcount to calculate how many people had died already? If someone died during the headcount, they certainly would not even mind, as they did not care about anything at all. Were they doing a headcount to make sure none of us had escaped? There was no escaping that place though.

Everything done there and in other concentration camps followed an industrial precision, so everything would work like a well-oiled machine. The amount of trains deporting people, the number of prisoners, the procedures at each camp, and even the mistreatment of those incarcerated—it was a large-scale factory of atrocities.

Everything done there and in other concentration camps followed an industrial precision, so everything would work like a well-oiled machine.

When we arrived at Bergen-Belsen, Commander Adolf Haas was in charge of it all. Prior to working there, Haas had run the Niederhagen Camp, one of the smallest Nazi concentration camps. It was closed in 1943 and Haas was assigned to Bergen-Belsen then. You can see that the Holocaust was only possible due to the number of people involved in the operation. When we talk about the Holocaust and the Nazis, the first thing that comes to mind is Adolf Hitler, the leader of it all. However, each piece of the puzzle had its role to play, so that everything would work correctly. For example, Joseph Goebbels, the Propaganda Minister, was also an extreme antisemite. He was the one responsible for spreading the ideas of the Nazi Party throughout Europe, including hatred towards Jews. Hitler would not have done it all by himself: for this horror to take root, it took millions of blind people who were indoctrinated by the Führer's ideas—and sometimes these ideas resonated with their own.

Bergen-Belsen was not an extermination camp but its conditions did not allow for survival either. What do we need to survive? Proper food and good hygiene. Neither was available in Bergen-Belsen or any other concentration camp. Their intention was to wear out people little by little, so they would not have any strength left to live.

There was enough food at Westerbork for us not to go hungry, but the situation changed in Bergen-Belsen, where we were only fed once a day—if we were fed at all. Whenever we were given food, we needed to queue up to receive the little ration available, which was usually some sort of turnip soup and a chunk of bread. We had to get used to not having a proper meal for quite some time.

Only those who have experienced malnourishment can understand its effect on the human body. You lose your strength, you feel weak, and start to wither. Whenever I could, I tried to stay close to my mother, my father, and my brother. I noticed we were looking haggard, as was everyone else around us. Human beings do not know for sure how long they can survive without food and, at the same time, find themselves doing whatever they can in order to eat. These events allow you to learn so much about the human spirit and their ability to fight for survival.

Since we did not have much to eat, I remember we talked about food a lot in the camp. Prisoners would gather and dream about what they would eat once they left that place—enormous banquets were often mentioned. Some had memorized recipes. That was a way to escape the cruel reality, even if only for an instant, and believe that there could be life after that place once again, a life we could only dream of.

Spending time with children was another way of trying to escape reality. Helping take care of them and telling them stories, so they could dream as well, was a way to help yourself. Many women took care of children, especially those who had become orphans. All this care, however, did not prevent them from being traumatized. No matter how young they were, they still had the sensibility to register what was going on there.

Besides the lack of food, another critical situation in Bergen-Belsen was the lack of hygiene. Latrines were dirtier each day as more people arrived at the camp. Whenever those latrines come to mind, I get extremely nauseated and feel complete aversion to them. It may seem hard for someone with a clean, proper bathroom to imagine what it was like, but think about a huge number of people using the same dirty latrine day in and day out. The foul, acidic smell was unbearable, but we still had to learn to live with it. There was not any soap for us to take a shower and try to feel a little cleaner either.

Lack of hygiene is something that robs any human being of their dignity. When you are forced to live in such an environment, you feel completely humiliated. All that filth around us showed us what we were worth: zero! We were nothing. Worse yet, we were parasites in Nazi society, and they treated us as such.

Despite the psychological aspect, it affected our bodies as well. Our health was clearly worsened by the precarious hygiene and the lack of nutrients. Every concentration camp was a den of disease and Bergen-Belsen was not any different.

> ***Lack of hygiene is something that robs any human being of their dignity. When you are forced to live in such an environment, you feel completely humiliated.***

There was a lice infestation, but those were not simple cases of head lice. Our degradation was such that prisoners had lice all over their body. It was a horrible feeling to have those nagging insects crawling all over your body with no intention to leave you alone. Body lice infest clothes, sheets, and blankets, and they are attracted by lack of regular showers. Concentration camps were a very fertile environment for their proliferation.

Since lice infestations are very uncomfortable we tried to stay clean with the little resources we had. I remember we used to spend a lot of time trying to remove lice from our clothing. It really took a long time because you needed to hunt those little creatures down and remove them with your bare hands.

Lice was just one of our worries in that scenario. There were several other diseases spreading through the camp and worsening the health of prisoners. Added to the lack of hygiene, many prisoners had diarrhea too. If diarrhea is inconvenient under normal circumstances, imagine what it was like under those conditions. I did not have diarrhea then, but my mother had it a few times. Can you imagine being in that situation and having to stand there for a headcount, not knowing how long it would take? There was no compassion, and that is exactly what they wanted: to remind us that we represented nothing, we were nothing, and we had no rights.

Besides diarrhea, many prisoners had typhus as well. That is another disease associated with lack of hygiene and crowded spaces, among other factors. Typhus made people very weak. The ill had headaches, were indisposed, and felt nauseated. I remember there was a large field near the camp and the Nazis did not allow any prisoner to set foot there. They wanted to prevent diseases from spreading to the population nearby, because diseases should only affect "filthy parasites," not specimens of the Aryan race.

Obviously, we did not have any adequate medical treatment. All we could do was hope we did not get sick in that place, which was almost impossible due to the conditions we were living in. And, if you did get sick, all you could do was hope you would get better soon. On top of living through war, which already made food and medicine scarcer each day, we were living in a concentration camp. Medication was a luxury item, since we did not even have food to eat.

Watching as people changed day after day in the camp was a dreadful experience. As time went by, everyone was rotting away before our eyes. It was as if humanity was being taken away from us, bit by bit. Every day, everyone was getting weaker, thinner and sicker. We were completely hopeless and left to our own devices.

It was as if humanity was being taken away from us, bit by bit. Every day, everyone was getting weaker, thinner, and sicker. We were completely hopeless and left to our own devices.

Our lack of hope increased each day because we did not have any news about what was going on. We were shut off from the world without any contact with the outside, any news at all. There was no radio, newspaper or anything. The little we knew was what new arrivals would tell us. We lived day after day in that same situation, without any information about when things would change, or any hope of leaving that place.

We did not know, for example, that war was still raging in 1944— more intensely than ever. Axis Power troops, composed by Germany, Italy and Japan, were fighting all over European territory against the Allied Forces, composed by the United States, the United Kingdom and the Soviet Union. Brazil joined the war that same year. In July, Brazilian privates arrived in Italy to fight next to the Allied Forces. Brazilian soldiers defeated the Germans in strategic cities throughout Italy and would later assist in liberating the Italian nation in April 1945.

While the war was still being fought outside there would be no sign of prisoners being released from Bergen-Belsen. That place was a huge black hole for me. People started to die due to the precarious living conditions, and I constantly feared for my life and my family. We lived with death and we could not help but wonder whether we would be the next corpse being taken to the crematorium. Somehow, we had to survive.

In this desperate, depressing scenario, prisoners tried to stay united as much as they could. Since the Germans harassed us and tried to put an end to our lives, we did just the opposite and helped each other. There was a sense of community among prisoners, especially those who came from the same country. We looked out for one another whenever possible.

Every day was a battle for survival. However, it was the kind of battle we really did not know how to fight. We were living in a fabricated reality without the right to react. There was no alternative but to keep moving forward and avoid trouble. We were living in the dark, blind, because we never knew what the Nazis were thinking—you could just be standing there, and it was enough to bother them. It is hard to explain; our being alive was something that bothered them.

The *Schutzstaffel*, known as the SS, seemed to enjoy the role they had been given. The paramilitary troops did everything they could to make our life a living hell in that place. Whenever they had to talk to one of us, they resorted to insults, humiliation and threats. We could not demand to be treated with dignity, there was no way of doing that. We had to accept that kind of treatment if we wanted to stay alive.

What shocked us the most was that the Nazis kept a clear conscience while resorting to brutality, because they truly believed they were doing a good deed in the name of Germany.

What shocked us the most was that the Nazis kept a clear conscience while resorting to brutality, because they truly believed they were doing a good deed in the name of Germany. Society should be alarmed when ideology becomes so deep seated that it supports barbarians with such an abominable purpose.

One of the tactics that they constantly used to torment us was to make us switch barracks all the time. There was simply no explanation for that: they would let us know, in their own unpleasant way, that we were supposed to collect our belongings and go wherever they were sending us to. Still, we could not leave until everything was organized just the way they wanted, according to their rules.

It was really inconvenient whenever they did that. Besides spending hours standing there for the headcount, subject to constant threats, and dealing with the lack of food and hygiene, we were sent left and right as if something was about to change, but nothing really happened. We were under constant stress and each moment seemed more challenging than the moment before.

I did not know, nor could I have ever imagined, but my father's nerves were wrecked. He started to exchange food for cigarettes; he would not eat the little he had so he could smoke. This type of black market was something very common in concentration camps. Since there was no way of leaving that place, prisoners exchanged whatever valuables they had. Food was a luxury item in Bergen-Belsen, so if you wanted clothes, for example, you would have to collect a lot of food to give in exchange. In my father's case, he decided that the most important thing for him was to smoke.

Nazis also inflicted suffering on prisoners with forced labor. My parents, my brother and I did not have to work because we were on the Palestine List. Eventually, I would do some work outside the barracks, either painting or fixing something in the precarious structure. Other prisoners had jobs that were a true torment. Jewish people had to complete absurd, pointless tasks; otherwise, they were punished. For example, they had to carry rocks and pile them up on one side, just to pick them up again and return them to their original position.

Jewish people had to complete absurd, pointless tasks; otherwise, they were punished. They had to carry rocks

***and pile them up on one side, just to pick them up again
and return them to their original position.***

Those who were forced to work had to do so to their exhaustion, hours on end, without minimal adequate conditions. Even though ours was not an extermination camp with a gas chamber that would decimate people upon their arrival, the conditions there were so terrible that prisoners were slowly worn out. The purpose was to make us die little by little, and there were plenty of reasons for that to happen.

Soon after our arrival at Bergen-Belsen, my aunt and uncle and my two young cousins were sent there as well. This "uncle," was actually my father's cousin. His daughters were so little and helpless—they were one and seven at the time—but were already suffering with that horrible situation. Some of those children were so young, we wondered if they understood anything at all, if that experience would stay with them forever. Years later, we have been able to confirm that those children grew up to be traumatized adults.

I did not know it at the time, but a girl who had gone to Jewish school with Anne Frank and me had also been sent to Bergen-Belsen. Her name was Hannah Elisabeth Pick-Goslar, or "Lies Goosens" as she was identified in *Anne Frank's Diary*. She had been to Westerbork with her father and little sister before they were deported to Bergen-Belsen. She was at another camp and we never got to see each other.

There was one time when my mother met a rabbi who could have been a relative. I remember they spent a long time discussing whether they belonged to the same family tree and, in the end, they came to the conclusion that they were related. My mother and the rabbi agreed that they shared some similarities from the David's lineage. Later on, I found out that the rabbi's family was based in Spain during the Inquisition. My mother's family was big and part of it was based in England, while others lived in Holland, and some were in South Africa where she had been born.

Despite of it all, religion was present in the camp. It was interesting to realize that there were two paths that religious people could take: they would either become fervent Jews and keep their practices and devotion, or they would discredit God altogether and stop believing in a higher power.

It was very common to see that, after living in a concentration camp, people started to deny God's existence. Faced with all that suffering, faced with everything that had been happening to the Jewish people and other minorities considered inferior by the Germans, many people wondered: Where is God? Why did He let this happen? How could we still have faith after witnessing all that? These were certainly feasible questions to those who were suffering.

> *Faced with everything that had been happening to the Jewish people and other minorities considered inferior by the Germans, many people wondered: Where is God? Why did He let this happen?*

Even though the Jewish people were the main victims of the Nazi hate and the system of destruction they had been orchestrating, we were not the only ones suffering. Back then, other so-called "Enemies of the State" were persecuted and sent to camps. Hitler used to say that war was the perfect time to exterminate the "incurable sick." The Nazis made the most of World War II to push the idea of a "superior race," an ideology that was loaded with all kinds of prejudice.

In addition to communists—Hitler's political enemies—gypsies were also considered an inferior race. Just like the Jewish had faced antisemitism, gypsies were the target of prejudice prior to the War. Jehovah's Witnesses, a group that preaches about Christian principles from door to door, believed in political neutrality and, consequently, did not agree with the military service, much to Hitler's dissatisfaction.

Homosexuals were also sent to concentration camps because they were seen as "abnormal." In June 1935, the Nazi State decreed that the mere friendship between two homosexual men was considered a crime. It is very ironic that all these atrocities were committed based on laws that had been enacted and followed. What kind of laws are those?

People with physical and mental disabilities were also included in the group of the "incurable sick" who should be eliminated, according to the Nazi doctrine. That is why many disabled individuals were considered a burden on society and executed by the Nazis with the aid of German doctors. It is frightening to realize that Hitler had so much support to put such an evil plan into action.

The Nazi State came to power with a radical discourse and attitude from the very beginning. It was clearly built to put an end to diversity and control people through a dangerous ideology. Those acts of horror that the Nazis were implementing had been largely accepted and supported by the vast majority of the German population, all for the sake of economic growth. My life in Bergen-Belsen and the nullification of the Jews by the Germans during World War II were consequences of this dangerous ideology. Did millions of people have to suffer and was it all worth it for the good of a superior Aryan race? Despite sounding absurd, many bought that idea and believed in it.

The idea of God was intensely questioned inside concentration camps. Even though many imprisoned Jews started to deny the existence of a higher being, many people were still devoted to their faith and religion. In Bergen-Belsen, some of the men tried to keep praying and following the Jewish calendar. It became more of a challenge as we started to lose track of what day it was.

Since there was not a calendar we could not tell what day of the month or the week it was. Even though we knew the exact date of our birth, we could not really celebrate it. How could we celebrate someone's birthday when there were more chances of death instead of life? People passed away and we did not even have time to mourn; we had to move on and try to survive to see another day.

How could we celebrate someone's birthday when there were more chances of death, instead of life? People passed away and we did not even have time to mourn; we had to move on and try to survive to see another day.

Little by little, the Nazis stripped us of all elements of a normal life: education, money, the right to have a home and be free. In the camps, they also wanted to strip us from our humanity. Life in all concentration camps was so depressing that people started to dehumanize themselves. The purpose behind it was to make prisoners shrink into nothing. We were treated like animals, not like human beings. They wished to make us weak by denying us food; they wished to take away our will to live by making us witness all that horror; they wished to strip us of our dignity by keeping us filthy—and Bergen-Belsen was getting filthier by the minute.

They also tried to get rid of the concept of family. Even though family members were kept together, there was no assurance that all of them would be safe. They wished to instil selfishness in prisoners, make them become individualistic, so that we would not care about anyone or anything else.

In a nutshell, what the Nazis wanted was to strip us of our humanity, deny us the feeling that we were worth anything. Since they saw everyone in concentration camps as inferior, they wanted us to feel inferior. After all, how else would they be entertained if we did not feel as worthless as they thought we were? How else would they be entertained if we did not see ourselves as inferior as well? Day after day, while subjecting us to inhumane actions—be it physical or verbal humiliation—they wished prisoners would waste away until they had no strength left to survive. That was how they would reach their ultimate goal: to exterminate every single one of us.

However, despite adversities we withstood the difficulties and managed to survive. It was not easy for me and my family, but we found strength to carry on—I do not even know where this strength came from. In spite of it all, we were still alive.

That is how we spent our first months in the camp. They reduced us to nothing and denied us of everything we had accomplished in life so far. We did not know it back then, but the situation was yet to take a turn for the worse. From then on, we would have to withstand worse conditions. What could be any worse than lack of food and dignity? I could not answer this question then, but I would soon learn a lesson: Bergen-Belsen was about to show us what an unbearable place it actually was.

5

TOUGH LOSSES

Bergen-Belsen had few resources for prisoners to survive in the camp. While the Nazis had good food, warm clothes, and lived in comfortable houses, prisoners had to make do with what they had. The situation would get worse by the end of 1944, as the war unfolded and the Nazis and the SS implemented their strategies.

People were getting more debilitated each day. We had been in the camp for several months, suffering with a life of reclusion, anxious about how much longer we would have to live in that world, in that surreal situation. We were losing weight quickly and showing signs of malnutrition, which also reduced our mental abilities, weakened our immune system, and put us at risk.

Winters are unbearable in northern Germany, and the cold season was approaching in the end of 1944. We did not have any news about the world outside, but World War II was on its last throes. That was when the Allied troops spread throughout the territory that had been occupied by the Third Reich. Part of the Soviet army was moving quickly into Eastern Europe, and the Germans were becoming concerned as the Soviet Union became aware of their crimes and witnessed the atrocities that had been committed in concentration camps, since some of the prisoners were Soviets. As for the U.S. and British troops, they were making their way into German territory as well.

That was one of the most cruel and intense years of the Holocaust. About two million Jews had already died. Throughout all those years in war, Jewish people were decimated in extermination and concentration camps, executed outdoors, gunned down at ghettos, and subjected to all sorts of savage acts perpetrated by the Nazis. Entire families disappeared during that seemingly endless war. It is striking and at the same time sad, that there are people who still deny that all of this ever happened. I am a living proof of all this brutality, which was not fabricated by my imagination.

> ***Entire families disappeared during this seemingly endless war. It is striking, and at the same time sad, that there are people who still deny that all of this ever happened.***

The horror was so real that, as enemy troops advanced, the Germans started to fear justice. After all, if the Allied Forces won the war, they would not let the Germans get away with destroying and occupying the European continent during Hitler's ambitious delusion to become the "Emperor" of Europe. Germany was already at a disadvantage. After World War I, Germany was held accountable and forced to sign the Treaty of Versailles, which imposed reparations that Germans considered damaging to their country, such as giving away some border territories, having a limited Army, and being banned from exploring economic resources in some German regions.

By late November—maybe they were already anticipating their defeat—Himmler issued an order to destroy crematoriums in some concentration camps. In an attempt to cover any traces of death and extermination at the Auschwitz-Birkenau camp, the Germans started to evacuate prisoners in 1944 and imploded some gas chambers, such as the one in Sobibor. As the Germans did not want to release their prisoners, some of them were sent to Bergen-Belsen in Germany.

That was when The March of Death started. For transfers to be carried out, prisoners had to walk for miles and miles, all along having our lives threatened by the Nazis. We were only allowed to rest when the guards told us so; otherwise, those who were unable to walk any further would be killed by the SS. Some people would be on board of those extremely crowded cattle wagons again. Many people passed away during these walks because they could not withstand it any longer; they just did not have any strength left in them.

Anne Frank and her sister Margo also boarded the train in late October 1944 to go to Bergen-Belsen. They were already very weak due to the conditions they experienced in Auschwitz, and that trip would not help the two sisters improve their health. They had left their mother, Edith, back in Auschwitz and no longer had any news about their father, Otto. It seemed like a never-ending war.

When the Frank sisters arrived at Bergen-Belsen, along with other female prisoners from Auschwitz, some tents became makeshift shelter at the prisoners camp—there was a serious lack of space at the time. They braved the worst of storms, which destroyed the camp where they were lodged in November 1944, and they were soaking wet all through the intensely cold night. They were only transferred to another place the next day.

We were unaware of those events, but would soon get to experience them first hand. We were getting increasingly more concerned, not knowing what would happen to us as life in the concentration camp went on—could we call it "life" at all? My mother always kept her hopes up though. She was optimistic about our chances of leaving that situation.

My father was not as hopeful; he looked more depressed each day. There was practically no food available. We were literally starving.

There were days when we would not eat at all. Still, my father exchanged the little food he had for cigarettes—and that was an exchange that could not lead to anything good.

Sometimes life seems to play some tricks on us just to see how far we can go. A girl my age does not expect to lose her father, her safe haven. The natural cycle of life is for a child to lose a father when he is elderly, when we are better prepared—that is, if you can ever prepare yourself for it at all. Once again, life would make me face a loss, and I would have to deal with it in order to survive.

One day in late November 1944, my brother came looking for my mother and me. He was very emotional and tense. He said, "Father is dead."

One day in late November 1944, my brother came looking for my mother and me. He was very emotional and tense. He said, "Father is dead." The only thing I could think about was that my dear father had left us. It was a terrible shock. We felt his loss deeply within our soul and in our already frail bodies. From the day I lost my little brother, I was aware that life is fragile and can come to an end at any moment, without any warning. However, you never get used to the idea of losing someone you love. There is no preparing for that.

My father had had a fatal heart attack and there was no way of saving him. Even if he had not died right after the heart attack, how could he ever survive without any medical attention? Without any medication and proper care? The absence of food, the cigarettes, and—especially—the humiliating situation that the head of our family had been subjected to, being unable to remove his wife and beloved children from a dangerous environment, had been his death sentence.

The absence of food, the cigarettes, and—especially—the humiliating situation that the

***head of our family had been subjected to, being unable
to remove his wife and beloved children from a
dangerous environment, had been his death sentence.***

I remember looking in the direction where his barrack was and seeing some men carrying his lifeless body outside. That image will be forever imprinted on my mind. We were reminded every single day that Jews were not human beings in the eyes of the Germans. We were but filthy parasites to them.

We did not even have time to mourn my father; that was unimportant to the Nazis, because our losses were actually their ultimate goal. We simply had to keep surviving through it all.

In addition to our pain, losing my father also meant losing the little privileges we had. We were on the Palestine list and had been sent to the Star Camp in Bergen-Belsen because of his influence and good position at the bank. After his death, there was no justification for such "perks," so everything was about to change. It is incredible how life can turn upside down in a matter of seconds. Could it get any worse? Could we ever go deeper into darkness? We soon found out, as things indeed took a turn to the worse.

It was around that time, early December 1944, that Bergen-Belsen would welcome one of the worst people to ever set foot at that camp: Josef Kramer, better known by prisoners as "The Beast of Belsen." Kramer had joined the Nazi Party in 1931 and later became part of the SS. He went through different concentration camps, such as Dachau, and had controlled gas chambers at Auschwitz-Birkenau before arriving at Bergen-Belsen.

Kramer replaced the former camp commander, Adolf Haas, who had left his leadership position to join the German army. Since battles were intensifying every day, Haas went to the battlefront and would not survive the war, ultimately dying towards the end of it.

Kramer was known for his cruelty and coldness. He used to say that, "the more Jews were dead, the more he enjoyed himself."

Kramer was known for his cruelty and coldness. He used to say that, "the more Jews were dead, the more he enjoyed himself." When he was asked whether he felt any remorse while watching his victims dying in the gas chamber, which he used to control, he said he felt nothing at all. After all, he was just following orders. He really lacked any sense of humanity. Prisoners were afraid of getting close to Kramer because they feared for their lives.

Another famous SS member who would go from Auschwitz to Bergen-Belsen was actually a woman: Irma Grese. Just like her male counterparts, female Nazis were known for their cruelty and coldness. Irma was known for these "qualities" and became famous because of the physical abuse she put her female prisoners through without an ounce of compassion. I did not hear about any of it back then, but they say—including British newspaper The Guardian—that Irma kept a lampshade in her bedroom that was made of human skin from all the Jews she had killed. There are no words in the dictionary that could ever express this level of sadism. Nevertheless, these were the people who became part of the Bergen-Belsen "staff" back then.

We could unfortunately talk about these events and people at length for pages and pages. Josef Kramer and Irma Grese were not isolated cases; they were part of a group that had been indoctrinated to kill in the most brutal of ways.

As a matter of fact, Bergen-Belsen was hell on earth. My father was no longer with us—and he would never be again. We had to stay united as a family more than ever in order to survive. It did not happen though. They did not allow us to support each other after our loss; we could not even remain together, as we had been so far.

We spent a few days together, when nothing seemed to happen, but then things changed again. In December 1944, my brother Bernard was shoved inside a train and taken to another destination. My mother and I were desperate. Having him around made it possible for us to know that he was safe. However, our weeping and despair were not enough to change the Nazi's plan. Bernard was separated from us and sent to the Oranienburg concentration camp, which was also in Germany and not so far from Bergen-Belsen. We could not get any news from there, but making him stay was not an alternative either. Many men had been transferred there during this chess game that World War II had become.

My mother was extremely nervous and desperate when she heard the news. The two men in her life had been taken away from her abruptly overnight. The next day, I would be taken aback by some more bad news: My mother would be transferred to Magdeburg, also in Germany. She was taken to a place where she had to work to exhaustion, under horrible conditions, at a factory that manufactured airplane parts. Her workplace was 765 yards below the ground.

Those were times of war and all supplies were essential. Back then, Germans used prisoners as slave labor in order to meet their goals in battle. Prisoners only had two alternatives: you were either killed by the Nazis, or you would work for the rest of your days to meet their needs during the war. And, if you did not do a good job, you would be eliminated, because you were not good for anything else.

I was feeling desperate and did not know what to do. It was the hardest time in my life. I did not know what had happened to my mother and brother; I did not even know where they had been taken at the time. I was all alone and could not even imagine what would happen to me. Just like them, would I also be transported somewhere else? I wondered if I would ever see my family again, if we would ever have a life outside Bergen-Belsen, away from that nightmare.

There was no time to feel sorry for myself. On December 5, 1944, I was all alone in Bergen-Belsen, without my family and uncertain about how much longer I would be able to survive—and how much longer they would be able to survive. The only thing I was sure of back then was that my father had died and I would have to do whatever it took to move on.

I would no longer be at the Star Camp and was transferred to the Small Women's Camp. There was no Palestine List for me now, nor was there any possibility that I could be transferred somewhere better. My situation only got more precarious, since things were even worse outside the Star Camp without any intention of exchanging hostages.

After I got transferred to another camp inside Bergen-Belsen, other relatives ended up dying due to the horrible conditions: my father's cousins had died and left their young daughters all by themselves. Had I heard about it then, were I close enough to them, I would have taken care of those little girls. However, that was not possible. I only became aware of what had happened after the war was over, when I was reunited with my little cousins. They were not alone, though; they had been taken care of by the Birnbaum family, who looked after orphan children at the Star Camp.

Even though my younger cousin was too little at the time—she was only one year old—all throughout her life it was clear that her time in Bergen-Belsen had had a wicked effect on her. We wondered if she was old enough to associate things or have a feeling of what was happening all around her. She started fainting suddenly and had psychological problems due to what she was experiencing. There was no escaping the wounds and the trauma; no one could ever succeed in doing so there.

I remember the camp that I had been transferred to being overcrowded. There were too many women on top of each other in the barrack I was assigned to, and there were more female prisoners coming in each day. How could we survive that situation, without any minimal conditions for the people who were already there, if more people kept arriving daily?

There were more transfers taking place between camps. The population in Bergen-Belsen increased each day. By mid-1944, there were seven thousand prisoners in the entire complex. By December, that number had more than doubled: we were fifteen thousand prisoners left to our own devices, trying to survive with whatever was made available to us. While the number of prisoners increased each day, the amount of water and any other bare necessities was decreasing. The Nazis would not make arrangements to bring in any more food just because there were more prisoners.

The decisive moments of the war were about to come, and the Allied Forces were more organized each day to defeat the Axis Power. However, there was no sign of relief or hope: the situation was getting more dramatic in the battlefield, especially in concentration camps, as more prisoners were being brought in.

Each new day in Bergen-Belsen was one more day to die, one more day to fight for survival. Being alive was already a miracle to me, after everything I had gone through. However, I would still have to fight a lot more before I could leave that place. When I was all by myself, that was when I went through the toughest time and had to look at death in the face. I had got so far, I would not give up living. The year 1945 would be decisive in my life and in the war.

Being alive was already a miracle to me, after everything I had gone through. However, I would still have to fight a lot before I could leave that place. When I was all by myself, that was when I went through the toughest time and had to look at death in the face.

6

REUNITED WITH ANNE FRANK

In January 1945, things started to become really desperate in Bergen-Belsen. I was constantly wondering if I would survive it all. If it had been hard to live there so far, it soon became impossible, because there was no room to take in one more prisoner and, still, more people were coming from other Nazi concentration camps every day. The same routine of headcounting sessions, abuse, and forced labor continued. It caused endless anxiety.

Being alone there made me change my perception in regards to survival. I could no longer count on the protection my parents and brother had to offer. Even though they had been as debilitated as I was, having them close made me feel more at ease and safe. Despite it all, my love for them was what kept me going. Now, I had to take care of myself, and I was increasingly concerned about falling ill or going through anything that would make me lose consciousness. Who would look after me if I were in that state?

Hygiene conditions were deplorable and, if there was already a food shortage when a reasonable number of people were brought to the camp, the situation became unbearable with the overcrowding.

Everyone was too debilitated to have any strength to withstand it all. That was why people were succumbing to these conditions left and right; diseases were permanent prisoners in the camp, too.

Each day about five hundred people were dying. This average made Kramer extremely happy, and he was proud of his team. I started to live among the dead; it did seem I was closer to the dead than the living. There were corpses everywhere and nobody was doing anything to remove them from the camp. Those of us who were still breathing were not that much healthier and more alive than those corpses in order to get anything done.

Crematoriums could not keep up with all the corpses that needed to be burned in Bergen-Belsen. Some prisoners had to push some bodies in wheelbarrows and dump them into mass graves. However, they could not keep up with the task either, because there were too many corpses around. Being among so many bodies was a living hell and I desperately started to wonder, "My God, will I be on this pile one day? Am I the next one to die and be left on the ground this way, as if I were nothing, as if I had no name?" The smell was unbearable; the stench of death and disease.

> *Being among so many bodies was a living hell and I desperately started to wonder, "My God, will I be on this pile one day? Am I the next one to die and be left on the ground this way, as if I were nothing, as if I had no name?"*

Prisoners were dying during the day and at night. It was common to hear the sound of death as we were sleeping. We would hear this frightening noise, similar to snoring, and we would know that someone had died. Their last breath before dying.

I went through this desperate situation and tried to survive another day, then another day, while waiting, who knows, for a miracle that would wake us from that nightmare. So far, there had been no hope that it would ever happen. We were not a priority for those fighting for the end of the conflict. Bergen-Belsen was a scenario of chaos that reflected a world at war.

On January 27, 1945, the Auschwitz-Birkenau camp was taken over by the Soviet Red Army, despite the resistance of German soldiers. After millions had been deported to that hellish place and exterminated in gas chambers, the Soviets were met by about eight thousand prisoners who were living in deplorable conditions. That was true of all Nazi camps.

Edith Frank had died early that January, after her daughters were taken away from her and sent to Bergen-Belsen. Anne and Margot did not know of her death and still had hope they would find their mother alive. Otto, however, survived and was freed from Auschwitz. Had Anne and Margot remained in Auschwitz and witnessed the Soviet takeover, would they have survived? We cannot say for sure; these are the facts. One more day at war does not bring you any hope; it is one more day to die.

Had Anne and Margot remained in Auschwitz and witnessed the Soviet takeover, would they have survived?

That was when I met my Jewish School friends. I was all alone in the camp, so being reunited with someone I knew was something that made me unforgettably emotional, because love and friendship were our only means of hope amid chaos.

One day, as I was walking outside the barrack area, I got closer to the barbed-wire fence that prevented me from having access to other parts of the camp. On the other side of the fence, I saw a face that looked familiar. It was Anne Frank!

Anne looked as frail as I did. I still had my hair, but hers had been shaved. I only caught a glimpse of her, since we were in different camps and I could not get any closer. However, that was enough to motivate me, to want to see her and talk to her. We would certainly have a lot to share.

I grew anxious about reuniting with her. It was frustrating to see someone you know, who could offer you some comfort under those circumstances, and remain physically separated by a fence, imprisoned and isolated. I wanted to fix that somehow, to be able to reach her, but going past the fence was suicide; it would not be possible.

Somehow, fate would arrange our reunion. The final throes of war were making the Germans a little disorganized. They were working hard to avoid liberation and, at the same time, they wanted to cover their tracks, as far as all the killing taking place at camps. In Auschwitz, before the Soviets arrived, they did what they could to disappear with the detailed records they had kept of everything that happened there.

One of the things they wanted to hide in Auschwitz, besides the gas chambers, were the macabre experiments that had taken place there—inhumane medical experiments that, in most cases, resulted in the death of "patients." Josef Mengele, known as "The Angel of Death" by camp prisoners, conducted his experiments in order to get a deeper understanding of the racial and ideological issues that were part of the Nazi doctrine. He injected ink into the eyes of prisoners to see if their color would change. He did horrible experiments with twins to investigate the issue of genetics in human beings. In Auschwitz, they also sterilized people in order to develop a massive, cheap and efficient method to prevent Jews, gypsies, and other prisoners persecuted by the regime from ever having any children. That was clearly another way to annihilate the "undesirables."

One of the things they wanted to hide in Auschwitz,

besides the gas chambers, were the macabre experiments that had taken place there—inhumane medical experiments that, in most cases, resulted in the death of "patients."

Fritz Klein was a medical doctor in Auschwitz and, like Josef Mengele, participated in the selection process—that is, he also decided the fate of those at a camp. He arrived in Bergen-Belsen in January 1945, along with other SS members who had a brutal mentality.

In Bergen-Belsen, they would also try to get rid of records containing information on prisoners and reports on all types of cruelty that had taken place there. Besides, there was also data identifying the SS members who worked there, which could be very problematic for them if Germany were really defeated during the war. Responsibility for everything that had been done so far would be on them.

Amid this scenario, I suddenly realized there were no longer fences around the place I was at. I could not believe my eyes when I saw it! It happened without any warning, no explanation at all. Maybe it was a sign that something bigger was changing the way the war was going, but the only thing I could think about was that I had an opportunity now to go look for Anne and talk to her.

I crossed the area that had been inaccessible to me until then and kept going. It was a limited sense of freedom, of course, but I could walk further than before. I had more room to explore, and I was determined to reach my goal!

I walked around the camp looking for Anne. Deep down, I really hoped I could find her; after all, there was a great chance she could be dead already, since it was not all that hard to die in that place. However, I kept my hopes up.

The same way destiny can place us before extremely different situations, it can also bring us gifts that are loaded with good omens.

Yes, I was in a concentration camp, debilitated, but meeting Anne was a great joy! And that was how fate, destiny took me to her. I could not believe I had found her, and that she was still alive!

And that was how fate, destiny took me to her. I could not believe I had found her, and that she was still alive!

I could not contain my anxiety and happiness, and I yelled, "Anne!" She heard her name and may have wondered where that familiar sound was coming from. She turned and looked at me with those eyes and that smile I had seen so often at the Jewish School. What an exciting moment! She had a blanket wrapped around her, because she could no longer stand all the lice in her clothes, and she was shaking because of the cold. We ran to each other and hugged, tears rolling down our cheeks. Those tears brought mixed feelings: they were tears of joy and relief for having found each other at that lifeless environment, but they were also tears of sadness for the depressing state we were in, because at that moment neither of us had our parents or any protection at all.

It is still a mystery to me that we were able to recognize each other: two skeletons in that place, amid so many others that all looked alike. But those familiar eyes did not deny our past in common, and there was no doubt we were there, together. We remained there for some time, holding each other, maybe because we needed human touch more than ever in that moment. We were not only hungry, sad, devastated; we were also clamoring for humanity.

We let each other go and had to catch our breath in order to talk. We had so much to tell each other! The first question I asked her was, "Anne, did not you try to flee to Switzerland?" It was odd to ask her that, considering she was there, in front of me, but when the Frank family disappeared and Anne stopped going to school, we all thought they had made it to Switzerland. There was no way to confirm that, so we believed it was true. That rumor was spread by members of the

Frank family themselves to have everyone convinced that it had happened, including those who were looking to get them deported.

Anne soon replied, "No, we did not go to Switzerland; we were hiding." Anne started to tell me about the secret hiding place, how life had been difficult there, too, that they could not make any indication that they were hiding to avoid deportation. Otto Frank had decided to flee with his family because Margot had already been recruited to perform forced labor. Since then, they were considered fugitives and could not let anyone know that they remained in Amsterdam.

Anne talked about her daily life in hiding: how they could not even flush during the day; that they had to rely on the kindness of her father's employees and friends who had helped them hide, so they could have something to eat; that they could not talk too loud or move too much within that hiding space whenever employees were working. In spite of it all, Anne was able to keep studying while in hiding and completed some distance learning courses.

Anne also told me about the diary in which she wrote everything that had happened in the annex. She listened to the radio, which they kept in hiding, so they could listen to BBC and learn about events related to the war. They had listened to an official address by the Dutch Cabinet Minister Bolkestein, who was in exile and asked everyone to put away their personal records. According to him, diaries would be published after the war, so that future generations could learn what had happened in Holland during that time. His address had Anne excited, since she already dreamed of publishing her diary and becoming a writer, as she had always wanted.

Anne also told me about the diary and that she kept writing about what was happening in the annex.

We stood there, dreaming about her book being published, about a reality in which she would become a famous writer, known for surviving the war, about a life away from that place for both of us. That was a magical moment and, for an instant, we were transported from that oppressive reality we could no longer stand, and spent a few minutes in a future full of dreams. Amid all that chaos we were still capable of dreaming.

Anne was also the first person who told me about Auschwitz—more precisely, the horrors of Auschwitz. Before our conversation, I could have never imagined what had taken place there. She told me about the cattle wagons and the selection process when people first arrived at camp, which decided who would die in a gas chamber and who would work like a slave in the camp. She also told me about the train ride to Bergen-Belsen. The two young dreamers we once were had now become two young girls who feared the reality we were facing.

Margot was there too. They were both very worried about their mother because she was still alive when they left Auschwitz, and they hoped to meet her again. They were apprehensive about their father as well, since they had not heard from him since Auschwitz and did not know whether he was dead or alive. Such was the unforgiving fate of many who did not survive to see the end of war.

I met Anne and Margot a few more times. We always talked about what we were going through. I told her my family was not with me anymore. Unfortunately, it did not take long until we stopped meeting. Fate would not allow us to comfort each other much longer; I would soon be alone in that place again.

I met Anne and Margot a few more times. We always talked about what we were going through.

One day, I could not find Anne. I heard from some of the women who were in the camp that she had not made it. Margot and her passed away in March, both from typhus. Margot fell from her bed and died on the ground—she no longer had any strength to stand up—and Anne died a few days later, also taken by the disease.

Some people argue whether Anne could have fought for her life had she known that her father was still alive. But how could anyone find the strength to keep living after that devastating disease, under those conditions? Could we ever say that everyone who died simply did not have any will to live anymore? That was not a variable of life in Bergen-Belsen. Survival was a matter of chance—maybe even a miracle.

Could we ever say that anyone who died simply did not have any will to live anymore? That was not a variable of life in Bergen-Belsen. Survival was a matter of chance—maybe even a miracle.

Anne Frank's diary was only protected and published because, after the family was found in their hiding place and arrested, Miep Gies—one of the people who had been helping keep them safe—found the diary among the belongings that the family had left behind. She decided to keep it and later had the opportunity to give it back to Otto. To this very day, nobody knows who reported the Frank Family. It was a very sad end to their lives, as it was for the lives of many Jewish people. Entire families were ravaged by war.

Lies Goosens, another friend who had also been in Bergen-Belsen, had been assigned to the Star Camp, but not to the same area where I was. We only found out about it when we were reunited after the war. Lies told me, "You were the only one who had a chance to give Anne a hug; I was not even able to see her. I could only talk to her through a fence and throw her some food." Yes, being reunited with Anne was very special and emotional.

Lies told me, "You were the only one who had a chance to give Anne a hug; I was not even able to see her. I could only talk to her through a fence and throw her some food."

Back then, the lack of food reached an unbearable, inhumane level. The Nazis left us without any food or water for days. However, they never stopped toying with us. One day, a cauldron full of mussels appeared in the middle of the camp without any warning. I was starving and could no longer go on without food. Still, I did not dare get close to it, because I was aware of how evil the Nazis were and all that food could have easily been poisoned. Even though I did not eat seafood because I am Jewish, I was fully aware that, had the mussels expired, they would not do me any good.

It was very hard to see that cauldron full of food while I was famished, and be unable to get any closer to it. Only those who have starved know how powerless and psychologically weary you feel when you are hungry. I had to be strong and wait a little longer. I had made it that far; I was not giving up.

Closer to the end of the war, it seemed death had decided to put me to a test a few more times. I went through some events that, to this day, I cannot explain, but I overcame it all somehow, and fate decided I should remain alive. Among all the experiences I had, two of them were very tense and took me to the edge.

Amid that chaotic scenario everyone was dying, but the Nazis kept doing their unbearable headcount, even when we no longer had any strength to stand up. I could not bear that endless nightmare—it was a bad dream we could not wake up from. During one of those headcounts, "Honorable Camp Commander" Josef Kramer told me to leave my place in that five-row group. My heart started racing, because that order could mean anything: he was going to kill me right there and then; he would draw his gun and shoot me; he could treat me in the most despicable ways imaginable. To my relief, or maybe because of my enormous luck, he did not hurt me or threaten me.

My heart started racing, because that order could mean anything: he was going to kill me right there and then; he would draw his gun and shoot me; he could treat me

in the most despicable ways imaginable. To my relief, or maybe because of my enormous luck, he did not hurt me or threaten me.

However, those few seconds seemed to last an eternity. There was nothing I could do, nowhere I could run to. That was my most vulnerable moment in my entire life: a victim waiting for her aggressor to decide on her fate. I could not breathe for a while, but nothing happened. However, that was not the only time my life would be in the hands of those brutal people. Actually, from the very day we were deported, my life had been at their mercy.

The other time death brushed past me was a more real and frightening event. The Nazis did not know what to do with everything that was happening during the war. They, who had been indoctrinated so well, were losing control of the situation. The Nazis deeply believed they were leading Germany to victory, that the Aryan Empire would conquer all, but defeat during war would put an end to their dreams. After everything that was happening, they could see that victory was more unattainable than ever.

There was this one time, really close to the end, when I was standing in line waiting to receive some water. I was standing there like a zombie, and so was everyone else around me, just trying to get some of the water they were making available to us, so I would not be more dehydrated. That was when I felt a heavy hand pulling me by the arm. I got scared, but I could not react, and that hand yanked me out of the line.

That was when I felt a heavy hand pulling me by the arm. I got scared, but I could not react, and that hand yanked me out of the line.

When I realized what was happening, my heart sunk. An SS member working in the camp was pointing a gun at me. I could never put into words how afraid and powerless you feel when there is a gun pointed at you—a gun that can put an end to your life. However, I did not have any reaction simply because I no longer cared. That man had a gun pointed at me, but I had already lost everything: my house, my family, my identity. They had taken everything away, and their taking my life was an expected end to it all.

I must have looked so indifferent, so emotionless before that brutal man that he probably did not get any enjoyment out of it. He wanted me to beg for my life, to be paralyzed by fear before him, so his *grand finale* would be to kill me. That was not what happened, though. He lost his bearings. He did not know what to do before an indifferent victim and, to make the most out of his moment of fun, he shot into the air. At least, he would not waste any bullets.

I think it was only after it was all over that I could grasp the dimension of that event and how I was inches away from death. It was incredible that I was still alive after all that; it was a miracle that I had been saved by my indifference. I cannot remember whether I went back in line. Maybe I could not even move after that.

The Nazis were not the only thing I feared; I was also afraid of having typhus, a disease as brutal as the SS men. All around me, I saw people dying all the time because of it. I knew that if I contracted the illness, I would be the next victim it would claim. After all I had been through, I did not want to be there, unconscious, extremely ill, suffering all by myself. However, we can never predict when and if it will ever happen.

The Nazis were not the only thing I feared; I was also afraid of having typhus, a disease as brutal as the SS men.

The camp was infested with people contaminated by diseases. In addition to typhus, there were also cases of tuberculosis, typhoid fever, and dysentery—which claimed an incredibly high number of victims. After the first months of 1945, thousands of prisoners died in Bergen-Belsen. It was a miracle that, despite it all, I had not contracted any of those diseases—at least, that is what I thought back then.

Soon the war would reach our camp. In February 1945, the Allied Forces met at the Yalta Conference to discuss the political configuration of the world after the victory over the Axis Troops—a victory that was becoming ever more likely. Germany was mostly occupied already and Germans showed signs that they would not withstand battles for many more weeks. That Conference was attended by Winston Churchill (United Kingdom), Franklin D. Roosevelt (United States), and Josef Stalin (Soviet Union). The Allied Forces were already planning to demand the "unconditional capitulation" of Germany, which was announced on May 8, 1945, and the division of the German territory into occupation zones.

Some territories had already been liberated from the Germans, as well as some Nazi concentration camps, as it had been the case with Auschwitz in January. Berlin had been bombarded and there were many signs of destruction throughout the city. Europe had been devastated on account of the war.

While all this was happening and their defeat was imminent, some SS members did not want to waste any time. Some guards left the camp to avoid being arrested by their enemies, and it was clear something was about to happen any day.

Their escape would not change anything or make any difference, considering our situation at the time. After all, we were not free. Resources were very scarce for prisoners those last few days before something effectively happened. We had no food and very little drinking water available. We wondered if we could hold on to life for a few more days until someone could finally come to help.

Hitler was aware of what was happening. However, he was so angry about his defeat and felt such animosity towards prisoners in concentration camps that he could not let it go. On April 7, 1945, Josef Kramer received an order to execute all prisoners in Bergen-Belsen, instead of handing us over to their enemies just to be set free. When the news reached the ears of representatives at the International Jewish Congress, in Stockholm, they pressured Himmler not to obey that order, and so he did, making Hitler extremely mad.

On April 8, thousands of prisoners arrived in Bergen-Belsen, which could no longer accommodate anyone else. Despite the lack of space, the Nazis kept taking desperate measures—they had their backs against the wall. Population in the camp had reached seventy thousand prisoners; seventy thousand people who would not be executed, but who would not be met with the best of conditions in order to survive. In a way, that was a mass murder tactic the Nazis were implementing.

Inside the camp, we were already wondering whether the war was reaching an end. We heard cannons being fired nearby, and we also saw the Allied assault squadron flying over the camp several times. U.S. and British aircraft took turns day and night flying around us. Bergen-Belsen was at the center of a war zone between them and the Germans.

Our anxiety increased at each explosion we heard. Something that made us desperate and outraged was the fact that there were no bombing attempts in Bergen-Belsen. U.S. and British air forces never bombed the railroad tracks or surrounding fields because we were not their priority. They were fighting a battle whose only objective was to put an end to German troops, not to save those who had been imprisoned in Bergen-Belsen.

Back then, I was skin and bones. I would look at myself and I could see the outline of my bones. It felt as if I were a walking skeleton wandering the world—a walking skeleton that would remain alive but for a brief sigh. Nothing in my appearance reminded me of the healthy girl I once was. I could not recognize myself. Towards the end of the war, I weighed a mere sixty-eight pounds, which was a healthy weight for a child, not for a sixteen-year-old teenager.

Back then, I was skin and bones. I would look at myself and I could see the outline of my bones. It felt as if I were a walking skeleton wandering the world.

Even though I was the right age, I was yet to have my first period. My body was not functioning the way it was supposed to. During the time we spent in the concentration camp, every woman had their menstrual cycle interrupted. I always wondered if that was actually for the better, since hygiene conditions would have been even more degrading for women without any sanitary napkins available.

It would take time for my body to get back to working properly. Life in a concentration camp had a very intense impact on my health and I would need more than a brief period to recover from it. The conditions to which I and all other prisoners had been subjected to were indeed devastating.

I was extremely debilitated; there was no time or willingness left for me to think about my family. The only strength I had in me was enough to just keep breathing. I was so weak I could not even walk anymore. I would spend a long time in my bunk bed, as most prisoners did when they could not take another step—especially those who were very sick. We all had that terrible look of death.

How come those planes did not come down to rescue us? How come the Germans did not just let us walk away? Why would they not leave us alone if they had already lost the war? The liberation of Bergen-Belsen was only a heartbeat away. Still, liberation did not necessarily mean survival for many of us. Certainly, our own personal war would never end. It would still take a long time for all of it to be over.

7

THE LIBERATION OF BERGEN-BELSEN

In April 1945, Germans and the British fought a battle in the surroundings of Bergen-Belsen. We could hear the sounds of war getting closer and closer. Those sounds may not bring happiness to many people, but for us in Bergen-Belsen, they represented freedom.

The camp was already completely infected by diseases—something that worried the Germans as the idea of prisoners being released became a more concrete possibility. What would happen to the German population living in the surrounding areas? The Germans would now have to deal with a situation that they had created themselves.

That was how two German soldiers appeared in front of the British troops waving a white flag on April 12, 1945. What could that mean? What was their intention? They had gone to the British to make a proposition: They were very close to a camp called Bergen-Belsen—a camp taken over by typhus. The German feared that, during a battle that close to the camp, prisoners could possibly escape and spread the disease throughout the population, even to soldiers, which included the British themselves—as if the Germans were worried about the health of their enemy. So the Germans wanted to propose a no-fire zone in the area surrounding the camp. In other words, that would be a neutral area where they would not fire their weapons, so the camp could be handed over to the British without any resistance.

That was the reason why many guards in Bergen-Belsen had already run away. They were aware of these negotiations taking place, and did not want to stay and be captured by the enemy forces. They had been brave enough to kill us and call us names, like "disgusting parasites," but they were not brave enough to face the consequences of their actions. The pact was signed by both parties, which meant that the fate of Bergen-Belsen was really starting to change.

The British did not believe the Germans at first. Would they really respect the no-fire zone? But they were not aware of the conditions they would find in Bergen-Belsen. Would those experienced soldiers of war be able to come to terms with what they were about to witness? Would anyone with the least amount of empathy ever withstand laying eyes on that hell on earth?

Would those experienced soldiers of war be able to come to terms with what they were about to witness? Would anyone with the least amount of empathy ever withstand laying eyes on that hell on earth?

At the entrance to the camp, the Germans had placed a sign that said, "Danger: Typhus!" Why would they put up that warning sign if they had created the situation themselves? They should have assessed the danger before they got it all started. They actually wanted us all to die of typhus inside, and they would not even need to lift a finger. Their purpose was our extermination.

The British were taken to the camp without having any idea of what Bergen-Belsen was. When they arrived, they used a megaphone to announce, "You are safe now. The Germans have left. Food and water are on their way. Please remain inside your barracks."

I can still remember that day as if it were today! Prisoners could barely believe what they had just heard. We would not be harassed by the Germans anymore? Could we have a different life from that day on? Despite being free, most prisoners in the camp did not have any energy to move and truly understand what was taking place.

When I heard that announcement, I was really weak and starving. I received it with mixed feelings. There were thousands of thoughts running through my head and I could not process them clearly. Well, I was free and could have a normal life again. But what kind of normal life would that be? I did not have my house anymore, I did not have my family. I was completely weak and my health had been affected. How would I live? Would I ever see my mother and brother again?

As soon as they entered Bergen-Belsen, the British were extremely shocked by what they saw. There were bodies everywhere. Most people were more dead than alive. The smell of putrefaction was unbearable. The terrified look in the face of those soldiers was the true translation of everything we had been experiencing in that place, where the Nazi indoctrination had sent humanity to.

As soon as they entered Bergen-Belsen, the British were extremely shocked by what they saw. There were bodies everywhere. Most people were more dead than alive. The smell of putrefaction was unbearable.

These were soldiers who had been trained to face extreme adverse conditions, kill the enemy, and save themselves from the worst of situations. However, not even those human beings used to seeing the sad images of war were able to believe their eyes, the degrading destruction they had found there. They certainly had no knowledge of Bergen-Belsen, and many remained in shock for quite some time because of what they witnessed there.

Josef Kramer did not run away like the other SS members. He remained there to welcome the enemy troops and "deliver" the camp to them, as if there were some sort of ceremony before the transfer of ownership. He was cold-blooded enough to explain the state Bergen-Belsen was in and nothing seemed to change the expression on his face. It was amazing to compare the lack of empathy of that man, amid the horror he had helped to create, and how the British could not believe what they saw or heard upon their arrival.

After field recognition was completed, the British returned to the entrance to arrest Kramer and the remaining SS members who were still there. *They* would be the prisoners from then on.

As soon as our liberators set foot in Bergen-Belsen, it became known as the "Horror Camp." The dehumanization of those still living was such that it was almost impossible to classify them as survivors. Bergen-Belsen would be forever known as the "Horror Camp."

Bergen-Belsen would be forever known as the "Horror Camp."

The scene was horrible, incomprehensible and yet, something needed to be done fast so that things would not get any worse. It was extremely urgent that they made arrangements to bring food and water—two resources we were in dire need of.

It was a challenge to those British soldiers who had only prepared themselves for battle. Now they had to deal with the situation they had just walked into. How could they bring any food for people who were malnourished? How could they bring life back to people who felt as if they were dead already, as if they were no longer human beings? They had not been trained for that.

Even though Bergen-Belsen had been liberated, it is important to keep in mind that we were still at war. Our reality was starting to change, but outside there were still shots being exchanged, cannons being fired, and it was hard to obtain food and medical supplies. There was no place they could go and easily pick up everything they needed in large quantities and in no time. However, the British soldiers dealt with the situation the best they could; their most pressing objective was to save the prisoners in Bergen-Belsen.

The day following the liberation, army trucks came in full of canned food that was intended for the soldiers.

If you think we all satiated our hunger, think again. We thought that too, but it did not happen. Since British soldiers were not used to fighting extreme malnourishment—or perhaps they were not aware of the extent of that catastrophe—nobody stopped to think that food could actually be harmful to us. Because of that food, many people ended up dying. Yes, that is exactly what happened: some people were so weak, their bodies could not withstand the amount of calories they were ingesting all at once. Many of them were starving and started eating so fast they could not even breathe. They died because their bodies could not tolerate what they were eating.

> *Some people were so weak their bodies could not withstand the amount of calories they were ingesting all at once. Many of them were starving and started eating so fast they could not even breathe. They died because their bodies could not tolerate what they were eating.*

The British troops estimated that about two thousand people did not survive eating all that food at once. How can you wrap your head around such a disconcerting situation? People had been deprived of food for so long, they had been stripped of any rights until then, and during their first moment of freedom and possible satiety, they died because of the amount of food they ate. It was clear that the consequences of living in a concentration camp were not restricted to the camp itself—those who survived it would carry that experience with them for the rest of their lives.

It was clear that the consequences of living in a concentration camp were not restricted to the camp itself—those who survived it would carry that experience with them for the rest of their lives.

Once again, I almost succumbed to the food. One of the British soldiers gave me a can of condensed milk and I ingested only a little, because I did not like the taste of it. I would probably not have survived to tell my story had I listened to my hunger and ingested the entire can. My body certainly would not be able to process all that sugar and calories in the condition I was in. Once again, I was lucky. Fate was helping me survive.

The situation in Bergen-Belsen was so precarious that, even after liberation, people were still dying due to malnourishment or diseases. Some were so debilitated there was no hope they would ever heal; they were just waiting for their last breath. That is what people whose beliefs show no compassion for others can actually cause to innocent people.

One of the British soldiers who participated in the Bergen-Belsen Liberation Operation was Leonard Berney. He was also Jewish and was twenty-five years old when he entered Bergen-Belsen without knowing what he would find there. What he saw was so shocking, he was never able to forget those images. Still, he was older than his fellow soldiers, whose majority had not turned twenty yet. Those young men had not even experienced that much in their brief lives and, from such an early age, they had already learned about the evil human beings can carry in their soul.

One of Berney's first missions in Bergen-Belsen was to restore the water supply to the camp, which had been interrupted by some SS members who ran away before the Allied forces arrived. As soon as he was able to complete that task, he was charged with many other tasks, because there was much to be done in the camp.

Now that I was free and alone, I started to think it would have been important to let my family in England know about my situation, so that I could get some support from them after going through that horror. I was not the only one in need of that kind of support; most prisoners had been taken away from their countries and needed to contact someone who could help facilitate their return.

With that in mind, I approached Leonard Berney one day while he was sitting at a desk and taking notes. I asked him if I could send a letter to my family in England to let them know that I was in Bergen-Belsen, albeit safe. He stared at me, perhaps surprised by how good my English was, since it was uncommon for people to speak English there. I gave him my aunt's address and he wrote a letter telling my relatives that I had survived and where I was. I have kept that first letter he sent to England on April 21, 1945. Funny thing is that he misspelled my name—he wrote Ninette, instead of Nanette.

Since I spoke English well, in addition to other languages, I started to help soldiers by acting as an interpreter in the camp. They found it hard to communicate with prisoners, since there were people from several nationalities and practically nobody spoke English. That way, my language skills in English, German, French and Dutch were extremely useful.

I have thankful, tender recollections of that man. After all, as a member of the British Army, he saved my life. He was one of those who entered the camp to free us, who were shocked and had compassion for our predicament—innocent people who had been subjected to the worst of punishments. On top of that, he wrote letters to help me communicate with my family. That was the first time someone offered me any help in months. It was a good feeling to remember that there were still good people in the world.

I have thankful, tender recollections of that man. After all, as a member of the British Army, he saved my life.

Another problem the British would have to face was how to deal with the large amount of bodies scattered all over the camp. The crematorium was in no shape to burn that many corpses, because there really were piles of bodies in every corner, since the Germans had not even bothered to take them to the ditches they had dug for that purpose.

The amount of dead people in Bergen-Belsen was impressive and frightening. When the British troops arrived at the camp, there were about ten thousand bodies scattered all over. That number increased, since people continued to suffer and perish. Some were so debilitated they would not survive even with the best of care.

When the British troops arrived at the camp, there were about ten thousand bodies scattered all over. That number increased, since people continued to suffer and perish.

Collecting the bodies was an intense, difficult task, because the British did not know what to do. They noticed that the Germans had started digging immense ditches, so they decided to resume that work. After all, it would not be possible to bury thousands of bodies any other way.

And who did the British assign to that task? The very same people who should not have even started it: the Germans. Some of the SS guards who were still there were forced to collect the bodies and place them in the ditch. It was impressive to see how indifferent they were while executing that horrible task. They did not show the least remorse about it.

SS members carried the bodies under the watchful gaze of former prisoners, who had been treated extremely badly by those very same guards. We were disgusted by it, but at the same time amused at that reversal of roles—now the SS had to obey orders. Germany had indeed lost the war.

It took them several days to complete the task. The destruction the Germans had caused was such that the efforts to repair it would have to be equally intense. It took them some time until the death rate started to decrease in Bergen-Belsen. Would things start to improve now?

After all bodies were removed from the area, arrangements were made to give those people a more dignified burial by bringing a rabbi to the camp. The British also called upon prefects and civilians from neighboring cities to come and witness with their own eyes the destruction that their doctrine had caused to humanity.

It was a striking view: thousands and thousands of bodies had been gathered, buried together, piled up until there was no place left for anyone else. The Germans watched it all and could no longer say they were unaware of it. Army photographers and cameramen registered the scene, so nobody could ever say that it never happened, so that what took place in Bergen-Belsen would never be forgotten.

Army photographers and cameramen registered the scene, so nobody could ever say that it never happened, so that what took place in Bergen-Belsen would never be forgotten.

Now that certain order and dignified conditions had been restored, the British needed to find a new place to accommodate former prisoners. After all, the camp was completely infested by disease and anyone would hardly be able to remain healthy there.

In the surrounding area, Leonard Berney found a place known as Panzer Training School—a tank school where German soldiers used to train. In addition to the enormous amount of food available there, the place also had plenty of space and comfort. The British were shocked when they realized that, so close to Bergen-Belsen, there was a huge amount of supplies stocked up by the Germans, enough to allow us not to go hungry. That clearly showed the deliberate brutality on the part of Hitler's soldiers. They starved us out of cruelty.

The British were shocked when they realized that, so close to Bergen-Belsen, there was a huge amount of supplies stocked up by the Germans, enough to allow us not to go hungry. That clearly showed the deliberate brutality on the part of Hitler's soldiers. They starved us out of cruelty.

The British got the Tank School ready for prisoners to be transferred there. However, some people were so sick, on their deathbed, that nothing could be done to help them. The sick were transferred to a makeshift hospital, while those in better conditions—which meant that they were able to walk—would be led to the recovery camp.

I could hardly believe that, after all those months, I would finally leave the concentration camp. Even though I was not going too far, it was liberating to know that I would no longer be in a place that reminded me of my father's death, my brother's and my mother's deportation, and all those horrible experiences I had to endure there. I would finally be able to breathe fresh air outside Bergen-Belsen.

Our transfer to the Tank School was initiated and soldiers were faced with yet a new obstacle: they were unable to organize the former prisoners correctly in order to take them to the School, because many small groups had been formed and people did not want to be broken apart. Considering everything we had been through, being surrounded by the people we had grown familiar with was something that brought us some comfort and security.

As for me, I did not belong to any small groups, so I did not mind that I would remain on my own. Actually, I could hardly wait to leave that place! I could not imagine myself spending another day there, now that being free was a reality. That way, I was one of the first ones to be transferred to the new recovery camp, because I was still relatively well and able to walk.

However, before we moved there, hygiene conditions would need to improve among former prisoners, so that diseases would not be spread any further. This way, soldiers improvised a "human laundry" —they sprayed a DDT powder solution on our bodies to kill all lice, then we went through the showers and they gave us a soap bar and a towel. Taking a shower felt wonderful! The water was so warm! How long had it been since I had felt hot water running down my body? Being able to use soap and a towel! What a wonderful feeling!

Taking a shower felt wonderful! The water was so warm! How long had it been since I had felt hot water running down my body? Being able to use soap and a towel! What a wonderful feeling!

Having the opportunity to take a decent shower was wonderful. Feeling dirty is degrading both physically and psychologically, and taking a shower made me feel like a normal young woman again. I was able to be clean and could even use soap and dry myself off with a towel—what luxury to all of us in Bergen-Belsen.

When I arrived at the recovery area, I went to work at the kitchen, where other prisoners had already been helping around. That place brought us a new perspective! We were among people who truly wanted to help and save us; people who did not think our lives were worth nothing, as I had been told every day of my life since September 1943. Now prisoners could feel human again, even though things were still so tough because of the traumatizing experience we had just gone through. Seeing people with an apathetic look on their faces was common those days.

My work at the kitchen only lasted a few days. What I feared the most had happened: I had contracted typhus. It is a silent disease, and you cannot foresee when symptoms will manifest themselves.

When it happens, it is intense. Incubation lasts for a couple of weeks, on average, followed by a very high fever. I went into a coma and became unaware of what was going on around me.

My work at the kitchen only lasted a few days. What I feared the most had happened: I had contracted typhus.

Like me, several other prisoners at the recovery camp contracted typhus and were transferred to a hospital. Those of us who looked healthy at first were not that healthy after all. Who could be disease-free after their time in Bergen-Belsen?

I am not sure when I finally woke up, but I was probably in a coma for about two weeks. When I came to, I was lying on a hay mattress on the ground. I do not know who took care of me during that time—all I know is that I was conscious again.

Once again, it was a miracle I was still alive. So many people suffered in Bergen-Belsen because of typhus, and so many of them perished, like Anne and Margot Frank. I had escaped death once more, despite the lack of medicine and adequate treatment. The odds seemed to be in my favor.

It is hard to say precisely how I survived while others did not. Did my body have more resistance? Had surviving it all been my destiny from the very beginning? During my time in Bergen-Belsen, I watched as thousands of people died, including my dad, and I always wondered whether I would be next. However, there I was. To this day, I cannot find a concrete answer; all I know is that I was really lucky all along and fought bravely to overcome all difficulties that had been imposed to me.

During my time in Bergen-Belsen, I watched as thousands of people died, including my dad, and I always wondered whether I would be next. However, there I was.

When I was recovering from typhus, Leonard Berney sent my family another letter to inform them of the state I was in, that I had fallen ill, but was being taken care of. The letter was sent out by late May 1945, when the situation was already improving for everyone in the camp.

On May 19, 1945, the last former prisoner was transferred from Bergen-Belsen to the Tank School. It was only after a month that the last people who had remained there could leave that place for good. It took many workers to make it all possible: British soldiers, medical students from England, and nurses from neighboring German towns—some prisoners despised the latter, since they were still German, after all. Despite not being fully prepared to be there, each one of them had to be strong and overcome the shock in order to help us. Nobody was ever fully prepared to what had happened in that camp of horrors called Bergen-Belsen.

Despite not being fully prepared to be there, each one of them had to be strong and overcome the shock in order to help us.

Since there was no way of maintaining the camp due to the horrible condition it was in, that place had to be burned down to the ground. Every barrack was set on fire and there would no longer be any trace of what had happened there. The last barrack was burned down on May 21, 1945.

The flames may have consumed the entire camp structure, but they were not able to erase from our memory what happened. Everyone who has been to that place, including prisoners and those who worked in the camp after the liberation, have never forgotten the site of destruction that the fire could never decimate.

Just like Bergen-Belsen, war was also coming to an end. Since the Germans could not resist anymore and their defeat was already a fact, Nazi Germany decided to surrender. On May 8, 1945, a

German Instrument of Surrender was signed to establish the capitulation of Germany. War, however, would only come to an end on September 2 that same year, with the capitulation of Japan, which had sided with the Nazis. On August 6 and 9, the world would still witness the American release of atomic bombs in Hiroshima and Nagasaki, leaving a radius of destruction in both locations. This was yet another example of how mankind can cause so much damage to the world, and how war is only good for one thing: to bring about destruction.

Now that Bergen-Belsen had come to an end, people were anxious to return to their homes. Some of them, however, did not have any wish to go back to their country of origin. That was true of prisoners from eastern countries, such as Poland. Now that the war had come to an end and the Germans no longer occupied those territories, Poland and many other countries fell under the Soviet Regime, which frightened them. They feared that, once back home, they would only be under a new authoritarian regime, unable to enjoy the freedom they had been dreaming of. Amidst this scenario, many people saw immigration to Palestine as an alternative to find a place to live, despite restrictions that had been imposed by the British authorities.

Even after the liberation, thirteen thousand people died because they could no longer fight for their lives. All the assistance they were receiving and the efforts made to save former prisoners were not sufficient to avoid the death of thousands more. After the Bergen-Belsen camp was burned down to the ground and closed for good, a sign was erected at the entrance: "10,000 UNBURIED DEAD WERE FOUND HERE. ANOTHER 13,000 HAVE SINCE DIED. ALL OF THEM VICTIMS OF THE GERMAN NEW ORDER IN EUROPE AND AN EXAMPLE OF NAZI KULTUR." More than six million Jews died in the several concentration and extermination camps and ghettos imposed by the Nazis. These are the official numbers, but considering what I lived through and witnessed, I have a feeling that the total number of people who lost their lives was higher than that.

More than six million Jews died in the several concentration and extermination camps and ghettos imposed by the Nazis.

After I woke up from the coma, I was transferred to a hospital in Celle, Germany, where I would start to get ready to rebuild my life. At the hospital, I was visited by another high-ranking member of the British troops wanting to meet the "English girl" who had survived. Leonard Berney certainly had something to do with it.

I was now getting ready to go back home. I was free and I could start over. I should go back to Holland, my country, but I had no idea what the future would hold for me. My father was dead and I did not know where my mother and brother were—or if they would ever be back. Despite it all, my general health was extremely debilitated for me to start living a normal life. Liberation might have meant that I would be away from Bergen-Belsen, but it would not bring peace and tranquility back into my life.

8

RETURNING TO HOLLAND

The Third Reich had really come to an end and the world was adjusting to a new order, even though the War was only officially over in September 1945 with the Japanese capitulation. Hitler did not want to face yet another defeat for Germany, after having witnessed what had happened during World War I as a soldier. Making a drastic—or maybe a cowardly—decision, he would not allow himself to be arrested by the enemy, that is, the Allied troops. On April 22, 1945, the Allied forces sent out a telegram recommending that Germans protect Berlin. Hitler already knew it was too late for any attempt to avoid his defeat. He and his wife, Eva Braun, had been hiding in a bunker and decided to take their own lives on April 30, 1945. Hitler shot himself in the head and she drank poison. Their bodies were taken outside, doused with petrol and burnt. That was the fate of the man who led the largest massacre in history against those who did not belong to the "pure Aryan race," according to his beliefs.

After leaving German territory, I returned to Holland with mixed feelings—anxiety, fear, and deep sadness. It was odd to return to Holland after everything that had happened. It seems that so many years had gone by since our life had been turned upside down. I did not know what my life would be like back in my country, or what I would find. Certainly there would be a lot of destruction, because most of Europe had been devastated during World War II battles. Holland had been liberated from Germany in early May 1945. By the end of 1944, the Allied forces had already joined combat to start liberating Europe. Before Holland was liberated in late 1944, there was a very severe winter that affected the entire country and was aggravated by the war—thousands of people who had not been deported, since they were not Jewish, died of hunger, cold, and diseases. That period has become known as *Hongerwinter*.

I faced a very difficult situation: I did not know what had happened to my mother and brother, we no longer had a home (it was confiscated as soon as we were deported) and my health was still extremely affected by my fight for survival. Nevertheless, I had to keep going. The time I spent in a concentration camp had come to an end, but I carried all the trauma and physical consequences of my time in Bergen-Belsen. Liberation did not make anything easier. I would still have to face many difficulties.

Due to my debilitated state, I was flown to Holland by the British Air Force, along with a small group of people who were in the same situation as I was. The authorities had realized that we would not be able to survive the journey by train in the state we were in.

It is in my passport, which I have kept to this day: July 24, 1945 was the day I returned to my country. I was taken to Eindhoven, in southern Holland. When I arrived, I was taken to a catholic school that had made arrangements to accommodate survivors. However, my stay there was very short; people connected to the school did not like the idea of receiving former prisoners and wanted the school back for the start of the school year, to be resumed soon. That was when I started to realize that people were not that interested in helping us.

After that brief stay in Eindhoven, I was transferred to Santpoort, which is closer to Amsterdam. There, I stayed at a sanatorium that had been prepared to receive concentration camp survivors. I would spend the next three years of my life in Santpoort, once again confined in a place with other people, but this time I was able to recover and live a normal life.

The sanatorium was located at an extremely bucolic area: the vegetation and tranquility of that place were typical of the countryside and very far removed from the agitated center that Amsterdam was. I remember we were often visited by goats, which would come to steal our food. I can still hear those goats walking around the building as if it were today. It was not home, but it was so good not to be in a concentration camp any longer!

When I first arrived there, I stayed at a makeshift infirmary, then I was transferred to another area. My bed was placed on a balcony, between two skylights. There were leaks in the ceiling and my bed was strategically placed between them, so I would not be soaking wet and risk having more serious health issues than I already had.

Even though I no longer had typhus, now I would have to deal with other illnesses: tuberculosis and pleurisy. Both conditions affected my lungs and my breathing. Because of tuberculosis, I felt extremely tired and weak, so I should be in bed rest most of the time. Tuberculosis cannot be cured quickly, and that was why I needed to spend so much time at the sanatorium to recover.

Being there was distressing, because I could not go on with my life or try to find out what had happened to my relatives. Were my mother and brother still alive? Would I ever get part of my family back? I was determined to learn what had happened to them, because any news I could get would define how I would live my life from there on.

Were my mother and brother still alive? Would I ever get part of my family back?

After camps were liberated, there was an intense flow of people throughout Europe. Some were trying to return home; others were looking for a place where they could start anew; most wanted to be reunited with the rest of their family. The Red Cross was making an enormous effort to share information about relatives who had passed away, even estimating possible dates of death. However, millions of people lost their lives during World War II—six million of them were Jewish. Can you imagine the communication problems that ensued? Europe was trying to restructure itself again amid a kind of chaos that did not seem organizable due to its proportions.

While some went home, others sought justice. In September 1945, a court led by the British in Lüneburg, Germany, started to judge the crimes that had been committed in Bergen-Belsen. Several individuals who had played an active part in the atrocities that took place in the camp were sentenced to death, including Josef Kramer and Irma Grese. As shocking as it may sound, those criminals continued to argue that they had not done anything wrong, since they were only following orders. How can the death of millions of people ever be justified as "orders that needed to be followed?"

As shocking as it may sound, those criminals continued to argue that they had not done anything wrong, since they were only following orders.

When questioned whether she had been compelled to torture prisoners, Irma Grese answered objectively: "No!" She also denied she felt any remorse for her actions. She was sentenced to death by hanging at twenty-two years of age. When the time came for her execution, her last word was "*Schnell!*"—"Quick!" in German.

Irma Grese was sentenced to death by hanging at twenty-two years of age. When the time came for her execution, her last word was "Schnell!"—"Quick!" in German.

It may be hard to comprehend, but I had already felt that I would never see my mother or my brother again. I needed something concrete to confirm that feeling, but deep down I was certain of what would happen. I remember I had a dream once in which I practically got what I needed. I dreamed my family had been reunited: my father, my mother, my brother and I. However, at a certain point, I walked in one direction while my family went the other way. That dream was telling me that I was alone in the world.

Soon enough I received a confirmation that would make me lose all hope of being reunited with them. Yes, all evidence pointed to the fact that I would never see my mother again. Still, maybe I was being stubborn and not listening to reason, hoping one day my mother would suddenly appear at the sanatorium with my brother to come and pick me up.

All my hope was lost the day I received the sad news from a friend of the family. He had a business in Sweden and went there looking for information about his relatives. As he researched what had happened, he met two women who had been with my mother and confirmed her death. That was how you were able to get news from your relatives after liberation: retracing possible steps and going after people who could share whatever information they had. Official organizations could not keep up with all that death.

In April 1945, my mother had been working under very poor conditions at a factory that made aircraft components in Magdeburg. As the end of the war was near and the Germans started to transfer people around, two thousand women who had been working at that factory were put on a train on April 10, 1945 and left without a destination. Eventually, the train arrived in Sweden, but my mother never made it there. The official date of her death was April 10, 1945. However, she died a few days after the train left the station, because she had no strength left. That was what those women told my father's friend. I do not know what happened to my mother's body, so I never had a chance to say goodbye to her.

I do not know what happened to my mother's body, so I never had a chance to say goodbye to her.

As for my brother's death, I never learned what really happened, as I got no confirmation about it. I can only imagine that SS soldiers executed him as soon as he arrived at the Oranienburg Camp, where he had been deported to one day before my mother left. His body was probably dumped in a mass grave. Even though I researched the camp records, I was unable to confirm anything. There is no record of my brother's death; it is as if he had never existed. The only certainty I had was that I would never see him again. My family had been destroyed completely.

When I had a clear perspective of the situation, it almost drove me to madness. I was weak, ill, and no longer had a family. Where would I go from there? How could I possibly survive alone, without any money, in a world that was not friendly to Holocaust survivors? Would I ever have the strength to carry all that weight on my shoulders?

I was really depressed about my situation, but soon I realized being depressed would not do me any good. Sitting there, complaining about my life and everything that had happened to me would not solve my problems. Besides, who would want to talk to a crazy orphan? I would certainly not be able to re adapt if I kept acting that way. That was when I soon recovered and decided not to be a victim of the circumstances. I had already survived, in spite of it all, so I would not give up and would keep on fighting to regain control of my destiny. After all, even though my teenage years had mostly been wasted and my family was gone, I was still a sixteen-year-old young woman.

That was when I soon recovered and decided not to be a victim of the circumstances.

Since I practically had no family in Holland and was underage, I needed to have a female and a male guardian. They were both old friends of my family. From the very beginning, they helped me and were very loyal. I remember the several times my male guardian went to visit me at the sanatorium. It was cold, and I would always say, "Sir, you better come in." After all, my bed was on a balcony. He would always say no, though. "If it's good enough for you, it's good enough for me." He was very supportive whenever he went to visit me. He really helped me immensely!

He also helped me manage the little money I had been given. The Dutch Government did not help any of the survivors and nobody provided us any assistance, even though all our property had been confiscated—I mean, stolen from us. Apparently, no one was aware of the situation, so we had to just make do. I received a very small allowance from the bank, which was my right because of the work my father had done for the company. It was really a small contribution, a symbolic gesture, but it helped to pay for my expenses at the sanatorium to make up for the time I spent there.

The Dutch Government did not help any of the survivors and nobody provided us any assistance.

We did not have much to do to pass the time at the sanatorium. We could stand for a few minutes, but I was on bed rest most of the time, so I could recover from tuberculosis. In order to pretend that time was not going by as slowly as it seemed, I used to write letters. There was also a radio that could be turned on during certain hours of the day—there was no broadcast TV back in the day. When we were supposed to rest, the radio would be turned on, but during all other times, the other survivors and I could only dream about the notes that came out of the device. In addition to that, I was able to read some books I had been given.

Besides visits from my male guardian, I was also visited by other people at the sanatorium. I remember that one of the first people who came to see me when I was still in Eindhoven were some soldiers from the Jewish Brigade. They came to visit close to Rosh Hashaná, the Jewish New Year, which is a religious holiday we celebrate in the end of September, when Jewish people must reflect on their actions during the previous year.

In October 1945 I received a wonderful surprise: Otto Frank sent me a letter at the sanatorium, saying he wished to come and visit.

In October 1945 I received a wonderful surprise: Otto Frank sent me a letter at the sanatorium, saying he wished to come and visit. Hannah Goslar had told him where I was and that I had seen Anne in Bergen-Belsen. Otto came to visit me indeed. I remember I was still very weak, and he got very sad, because he had found someone who could confirm that Anne and Margot had passed away in Bergen-Belsen.

During his visit, Otto told me that he had plans to publish Anne's diary, which Miep Gies had given to him upon his return to Amsterdam. It reminded me of how Anne had dreamed about that when we met in Bergen-Belsen, but she had not lived to see that day. Otto asked me what I thought of his idea. "Well, if you think you should publish it, you had better do it," I told him. The first edition of the diary came out in 1947. Otto kindly gave me a copy as a present. I lent the book to an uncle and never saw it again, but I remember that first edition printed in newspaper sheets.

It was really so sad that Anne was not alive to see her dream coming true. She had become a famous writer, as she always wanted to. However, only Otto could witness that moment. Many dreams were destroyed during the Holocaust, and there was no time for many other dreams to ever come true.

***Many dreams were destroyed during the Holocaust, and
there was no time for many other dreams to ever come
true.***

Another memorable visit I had at the sanatorium was of my aunt
from England. She wrote me in January 1946 letting me know she
was coming. I could barely contain my anxiety and joy in seeing a
relative again! My aunt was on board of one of the first ships to
transport civilians after World War II. I remember she was wearing a
military uniform when she came to visit, because she had been
working as a secretary at a Jewish military club in England.

Being reunited with my aunt was so thrilling and, at the same time,
extremely difficult. We did not have much to say since most of our
family had perished during the war. Our reunion represented what
was left of us.

The other relative I corresponded with was a cousin who was living
in the United States. I remember that one of the first parcels I
received after my time in a concentration camp was actually sent by
him. It was a "First Aid Kit"—after all, I did not have any belongings.
It contained a hairbrush, a toothbrush, some toothpaste... These
personal care items really came in handy. It was so good to receive
that kit, not only because those were practical items but because it
meant he cared about me. Whenever he could, he also sent me some
money to help me.

It was also at that time that I met a relative I had never heard of. One
day, a soldier wearing a kilt came to visit me at the sanatorium. He
said we were related and he wanted to meet me. The female nurses
grew very curious about that man wearing a traditional Scottish skirt
in the middle of the sanatorium and started following him around the
building. He introduced himself to me and said our mothers were
cousins. He was a major of the Scottish Brigade who learned about
my predicament through our family members in Belgium. He then
decided he had to meet me and convinced his superior to lend him a

car so he could drive to Holland. It was a really unexpected and funny event!

My new-found cousin's visit did not bring joy only to me, but to other sanatorium patients as well. He had brought supplies he thought I could use, so I had a full stock of chocolate, soap bars, and other presents under my bed. I used to organize everything and then share it with my sanatorium companions. One of my mother's cousins, who lived in Antwerp, frequently visited me as well to bring me food and socks she had knitted. She did everything she could to help me; she even brought her daughters to meet me, and I am friends with them to this very day. All those visits provided us such good memories.

Those were little moments of joy amid the bleakness I had experienced those past few years and what I was still going through at the sanatorium. I did not get many more visitors, since most of my extended family was Jewish and had been exterminated. However, these little actions of kindness, like the kilted cousin who drove all the way to Holland to meet me, made my days brighter.

> *I did not get many more family visitors, since most of my extended family was Jewish and had been exterminated.*

I met my cousin again in 1972, when I went to Israel. I remember he was speechless when he saw me; all he could do was hug me. He could not believe that frail girl he had visited at the sanatorium had survived and regained her health. He looked at me as if I were a miracle—maybe I really was.

Other sanatorium patients were concentration camp survivors as well. There were patients from several camps, with several stories to tell. We used to talk about what we had experienced during our times of horror, which also contributed to my recovery.

At the sanatorium I made friends with a woman who was also Jewish and had been deported to Auschwitz. She used to work there extracting golden teeth from corpses in the concentration camp. One day, the Germans took her to a gas chamber, since they had no use for her slave work any longer. She was already inside the gas chamber, about to be killed, when the Soviet troops reached the camp. The SS guards became desperate and removed everyone who had been awaiting their death inside the gas chamber and put them on a train to be transferred to another camp. Her fate had been decided on a matter of seconds.

In Poland, the Holocaust was very bloody and desperate—not only at extermination camps, but because to what the local population had been subjected. This story reminds me of the time I spent at the Jewish School in 1941. One of our classmates was Polish, and her name was Danka. She had told me that the Germans were killing Jews in Poland by asphyxiating them with poisonous gas inside large trucks with air-tight sealed compartments. At that time, I could not believe what she was saying, but after everything I had been through, I know now that conversation was only a prelude to what was yet to come.

At the sanatorium I also met patients who had been in camps organized by the Japanese in Indonesia. It turns out concentration camps are not exclusive to Nazis in World War II. Indonesia had been a Dutch colony and, after Holland was occupied by the Germans, the Japanese invaded the country and created some concentration camps where they kept Europeans—mostly Dutch—as prisoners. The stories I was told by survivors from those camps show that the Japanese were just as brutal as the Nazis had been.

The stories I was told by survivors from those camps show that the Japanese were just as brutal as the Nazis had been.

The Jewish people have a strong sense of community, so Jews from neighboring cities would always come to visit. I remember it made non-Jews jealous. There was this case of a Jewish girl who was having problems with her lungs and, in order to save her life, members of the Jewish community offered to pay for her surgery in Switzerland, which unfortunately would not be enough to save her life. Since her death was imminent, members of the Jewish community kept her company until her very end and were present at her funeral.

Aalsmeer, the next nearby town, eventually made the sanatorium their cause and started to offer entertainment to everyone. I remember the concerts they planned just for us, which really made us happy.

It took me three years until I was well enough to leave the sanatorium. After roughly one year, my digestive system started to work normally again—before that, I had been unable to gain any weight. I remember it was an enormous accomplishment to go back to weighing one hundred and ten pounds again. It had been a struggle for survival, and I wrote to my aunt in England to tell her about my personal victory.

After such a long time I was anxious to leave the sanatorium and to have a normal life again. Sanatorium supervisors were reluctant when the time came to discharge me, because they said I was not in optimal condition to lead an ordinary life yet. On the other hand, I could barely stand another day shut off from the world—first in concentration camps, then in recovery. I had just about enough.

The time it took me to recover shows how brutally we were treated in Bergen-Belsen. It took much effort and patience for me to overcome all of it. Not only did I have to get past the psychological abuse, also the loss I experienced, the youth that had been taken away from me and the traumatizing events I had witnessed in the camp. I also had physical memories of the time spent there, which had devastated my body as if the horror could never leave me alone.

Back at that time, I exchanged some letters with a nurse who had lived with us to take care of my little brother who had died very young due to a heart condition. Since sanatorium supervisors were saying that I was not completely healed, she went there and said, "I am a registered nurse and if I cannot take care of Nanette, whoever will?" They released me, thanks to her, even though they insisted that I should rest during mornings and afternoons so as not to disrupt my recovery any further.

In order to verify whether I was really alright, the nurse took me to two other doctors to get a second opinion. Both said what I wanted to hear: "Nanette needs to have a normal life, ride a bike, breathe in some fresh air from the fields, and try to be happy again." I could barely believe I would finally live a free life. It was wonderful!

In May 1948, I went to live with the nurse, her husband, and their young son. They lived in a very beautiful place in the countryside, where I could walk and ride a bike in the woods. Their house was an enormous castle. After all that time without any privacy, I had a room all to myself there.

The nurse's husband was not all that happy about my being there and barely talked to me. He was a fervent Lutheran who used to read The New Testament every day after lunch. They went to church every Sunday and wished I should come too and play the piano, an invitation I would always politely turn down. Nevertheless, the nurse was very nice to me and would always take me out on strolls. I am very grateful for the way she welcomed me. Her support was crucial at that time, so that I could continue to seek a better life for myself.

Even though I was doing well, I could not stay there forever—nor would that be really possible. I was constantly communicating with my relatives in England and they said they wished I could go and live with them. My aunt came from England and talked to my guardians about this. They thought it would be a good idea. After all, that was the only close family I had left.

In December 1948 I went to England to spend six weeks with my aunts and uncle for a period of adjustment. Later, I returned to Holland and spent a few more months living with my little brother's former nurse. However, those would be my last months in Holland.

In April 1949, I moved to England for once and for all to start a new life.

In April 1949 I moved to England for once and for all to start a new life. I barely had any luggage. After the nightmare I lived through in Bergen-Belsen, I had to rebuild my life from zero and start all over.

Holland is my native country, the place where I was happy with my family and spent a good childhood filled with nice memories. However, it was also in Holland that the darkest period of my life began. That was the country where I had left everything behind, the place I returned to without my family and all else I had ever loved.

Now I needed to somehow live the rest of my life in another country. I was not sure how I could do it, but I was determined to fight and re-establish myself. After all, I had not gone all that way just to give up. The circumstances I had been in were a complete nightmare, but I would overcome it all. I would keep on fighting.

9

A NEW LIFE IN ENGLAND

I arrived in England with an entire life to build. I was only twenty years old, but six of those years had been taken away from me—a youth I did not have a chance to enjoy under normal circumstances. From the time Holland was first occupied, I spent practically nine years living in fear and anxiety. By the time I was twenty, almost half of my life had been dictated by the Nazi doctrine and its consequences.

Now that I would no longer live in my native country, I should start planning for an adult life after having skipped my teenage years. All of a sudden, I had to stop being a child to take on a mature posture. Now that I could plan for my future, my main concern was to support myself financially, since I only had the symbolic aid that the Bank of Amsterdam had offered me. Within this scenario, I could not depend on anyone, so I had to fight to earn a living.

I went to live with my aunts in Kingsbury, London. They had a simple, very small house, where I would be living with an aunt and uncle, who were married, and another aunt, who was single. It was tough; I was surrounded by family and could not help but think about my parents and my brother. It was almost impossible to overcome the pain that losing them had caused me. The pain was strong and it found a home deep in my heart, giving no signs that it would ever leave me alone. Forgetting it all and leading a normal life was unfathomable. All the time I thought about the events that had desolated me.

As soon as I arrived in London, I started to share a room with my spinster aunt. However, this arrangement had to be reviewed soon after my arrival, since she was an older lady who had been used to her own ways, and I was a young woman who wanted to read books and keep herself busy as much as possible; after all, sleeping made me dream of the horror I had experienced. So, I started to sleep on my own in a smaller room, where I could keep the light on to read and write well into the night.

I was not the only one affected by the loss of family members. My aunts and uncle were also trying to recover after the devastating trauma we had all gone through. Talking about what I had experienced in the concentration camp during the war was strictly forbidden in their home. If we never brought the subject up, I believe they thought we would deny that it ever happened, so Bergen-Belsen and those deaths would no longer be part of our reality, as if those events had not actually taken place. My aunts and uncle thought they would be protecting me by acting that way, but their behavior had the opposite effect. Being unable to share my thoughts with other people and tell them what I had experienced caused me much distress.

Those who never lived in a concentration camp will ever be able to imagine that you can leave the camp, but the camp will never leave you—you can no longer find peace.

Those who never lived in a concentration camp will ever be able to imagine that you can leave the camp, but the camp will never leave you—you can no longer find peace. All the humiliation that the other survivors and I suffered throughout those years was too unbearable to be left behind just like that. Some survivors went on with their lives and created new families despite their trauma. A few of them, however, were never able to deal with the pressure and ended up committing suicide. I had chosen life; I would keep moving forward, despite the heavy weight I was carrying on my shoulders.

Even though I was suffering because of that silence my relatives had imposed on me, I never judged my aunts and uncle for that. After all, dealing with the tragedy of practically losing their entire family during World War II was also very hard on them. They were living in a country that had never been occupied by the Nazis, but they also suffered the consequences of those events, albeit indirectly. My cousin, who was deaf, could understand me more than my other relatives and showed me much support.

My family's house in London was a traditional Jewish home—everyone really followed the Jewish precepts. In our religion, it is very common to light a candle for those who have passed on. Consequently, my aunt used to light a candle on the days she believed my parents, my grandmother, and other family members had died. I watched her as she did that, thinking that it would hardly do anything to help us ease our pain. "I think you should stop, or you'll end up lighting a candle every single day of the year, because we lost so many people," I told her one day that I could not talk about the war, but everywhere I looked in that house there was a candle to honor a dead family member, reminding me of everything that was being left unsaid.

Before leaving for England, I made an agreement with my guardians: I would return to Holland twice a year to visit them because they were after all responsible for me. During my visits, I was able to talk more about what I had been through, because I was among concentration camp survivors. What a relief it was to let it all off my chest! I remember when I was sharing a room with my deaf cousin, and she asked me, "Would you like to know what you say at night?" I used to have many nightmares with Bergen-Belsen as the backdrop. It was something that I could not shake off. Even though my cousin could not hear what I used to say at night, she had the sensibility to realize that I was having many distressing dreams. Nightmares had become part of life for all former prisoners. Our war memories were very traumatic and the Nazis had succeeded in stealing our pleasant dreams away.

Our war memories were very traumatic and the Nazis had succeeded in stealing our pleasant dreams away.

One of those times I went back to Holland, my guardian told me that the President at the Bank of Amsterdam—where my father had worked—had refused to send my money to England, as I had requested before I left. I was the only person who could take care of it, and the situation was indeed outrageous.

The worst part was that I really needed that money; no matter how little it was, so I had to figure out a way to solve that problem. I had to go to the Central Bank and talk to the President to release that money transfer to England. And, who was the President of the bank? Well, he unfortunately was no stranger to me... He was married to the attorney who had cheated my family, saying she could make arrangements to get a copy of my mother's South African birth certificate and, despite the fact that she took our money, she never did what she had been hired to do. Oh, he made a scene, as if he were so happy to see me. "Hello, darling!" he said, giving me a kiss. "What a sight for sore eyes!" Well, I was not happy to see him at all, nor was I willing to play that part, so I said "If you do not give me what's rightfully mine, I'll tell everyone what I know!" He did not kiss me goodbye, but my statement was enough for me to get what I wanted.

I have no idea how I mustered the courage to behave that way inside the President of the Central Bank's office, but I had nothing left to lose. I remember that, when I came back from that bank visit, my guardian looked at me and said, "I don't know how you sorted it out, but I know what you are capable of." I just smiled and told him he would not have to worry about my money anymore.

I arrived in London in April 1949 and my aunt thought I should study, so she enrolled me at the Queen's College at Harley Street. It was a school for rich young women who had finished high school—which was the complete opposite of my situation. I insisted with my aunt that I should get a job to earn money, so I went to Secretary School and got a diploma that would allow me to work as a secretary.

As soon as I graduated, I started to look for a job. After all, I would not be able to support myself with the little financial aid I was getting from the Bank of Amsterdam. I was determined to find a job without anyone's help, so I applied for a job at a bank, hoping that my diploma would be enough for me to be selected for the position. I got a job interview at the bank and the gentleman who interviewed me said, "We only hire people who have a letter of recommendation. Who have referred you to us?" How could I ever have a referral? Once again, I would not take anyone's help. I simply said, "I'm Dutch." The interviewer stared at me and when I thought he was about to say, "Well, have a nice day, then," he actually said, "Miss, when you walked through those doors, the Director and I made a bet: He could swear you were the daughter of Martijn Willem Blitz, with the Bank of Amsterdam. He would like to know whether he won the bet... Are you and she the same person? Are you Martijn Willem Blitz's daughter?"

There I was trying to get my first job on my own merit, all the while knowing how hard it would be. However, despite being aware that my father was very well known and respected in the bank sector, I was only able to understand his influence then and there. I simply nodded, to which the interviewer said, "Miss, the job was yours from the moment you set foot in this bank." After all, my father was enough of a reference.

After everything I had gone through in my life, I was determined not to ask for anyone's help. I knew I could only rely on my relatives and a few close friends. In that case, because of my dear late father, it helped me, even though he was no longer with us. Martijn Willem Blitz may have been the victim of a cruel fate, but his legacy still lived on.

It was such a relief when I got the job as a bilingual secretary at the bank. At least I would be able to earn a living. It was then my guardian told me to let go of the money I was getting from the Bank of Amsterdam and, in spite of it all, I still had to thank them for their "aid." I was outraged, but I did it for my guardians.

I soon started my job and with the little money I was earning, I could afford some "luxuries" to live more comfortably. The first thing I did with my paycheck was to buy a portable heater which is an article of necessity during London winters. I hung it over my bed, since there was not much space left in my bedroom. I also bought a small wardrobe, where I could keep the few items of clothing I owned. Those were my little accomplishments, things I was proud of doing.

I was living my life and things seemed to be changing for the better. Still, I felt like a fish out of water in London. In England, young people had very little information about what had happened to the Jewish community in Holland during World War II—or even in the rest of the continent, for that matter. Since information could not be spread as easily as it is nowadays, details of the Holocaust were still unknown to most people, as if it had never happened. Therefore, I felt as if I did not belong, nor did I have anything in common with that youth that had no idea what so ever what I had lived through. Young people were not even aware of those events.

Since information could not be spread as easily as it is nowadays, details of the Holocaust were still unknown to most people, as if it had never happened.

I did not have many friends back then, besides a group of young Jews with whom I used to go out sometimes. When I was not at work, I spent most of the time with my family, which was somewhat concerning, since I was about twenty-year's-old already. Therefore, my aunts and uncle started to encourage me to go out more and lead a normal life, which also meant meeting a nice young man with whom I could eventually have a family.

After everything I had been through in recent years, all the family I had lost, leading a normal life was very difficult to me. How could I just leave all of this behind me and pretend I was a regular girl in England as if nothing bothered me? Still, I did my best to please my relatives and not cause any trouble.

That was when the brother of a fellow Santpoort sanatorium patient —whose father lived in London—invited me to a meeting about Zionism that targeted young people I decided to go and make my aunts happy. I was not really looking forward to it, but I did not want to let my relatives down.

I left for the meeting, but I got lost on my way there. I eventually ran into a policeman, who took me to the right place. "Miss, you should get directions to go back home," he said, "so that you do not get lost once again, wandering the streets by yourself." After the meeting, I heard a group of people say they were headed to go to Golders Green, where there was a subway and bus station, from where I knew how to get back home to my family. "May I join you?" I asked the group, but then instead a nice young man offered to accompany me.

I accepted his offer, so I would not get lost again. We got to the station and as soon as we arrived there he asked me, "Do you have a boyfriend?" When I said I did not, he surprisingly and rudely answered, "Well, anyway you are not really my type." He was indeed a very bold young man, but this was not to be our last meeting. When I got back to my family's house, my aunt was anxious to know every little detail of her niece's outing that day. She asked me about the meeting and I told her I had met a young man, which only made her more curious.

One week later, as I was walking up Fitzjohns Avenue towards the Hampstead subway station with an uncle, who had come from Holland to visit a relative who was ill, I ran into that fellow I had met at the Zionist meeting. He ran after me and asked me if I were the same young woman he had met the other day, which I confirmed. We left it at that, but my uncle told my aunts I was having an affair of which nobody was aware not even I.

The young man soon found out where I lived and what our phone number was. He called me and asked me out; he wanted to see me that Friday night. It seems I was his type, after all... I told him I would not be able to, because in our family one did not go out on Friday nights, since ours was a traditional Jewish home and Friday was our Sabbath—the weekly rest day for the Jews. He did not give up and called me at the bank to ask me out again. I could not help it and asked, "You've really been investigating my life, haven't you?" I soon called my aunt to let her know what was going on, and she told me I should go out with him. If I did not like him, I would not have to see him again.

Back then, relationships were very different from what they are like now. You could not go out with anyone without your family knowing first—especially in a Jewish family. When my aunt allowed me to go out with him, she already had sufficient information to know he was worthy of her niece. The fellow in question was also Jewish and his name was John Konig. John was from a Hungarian family and had moved to England with his parents in 1935. In 1939, when the war broke out John's family had been offered to be allowed to return to Hungary, but his father decided to remain in England. They were not welcome in the country, but at least they avoided not being deported had they returned to Hungary, so they did not end up in a concentration camp or being gassed.

John was still a young boy when his family moved to England, so he finished school in London. He entered university when he was sixteen and graduated as a Mechanical Engineer. Just like me, John knew what it meant to lose family. When we met, his parents had already passed away—when he was just twenty he lost his father to lung cancer, then his mother died of breast cancer soon after.

Part of John's family had moved to Brazil in 1930 and since he was by himself in England, his relatives kept insisting that he should move there, too. We started seeing each other only six weeks before John was to move to Brazil—that was September 1951. He already had a one-way ticket when we met and was ready to start a new life in Brazil.

Getting a Brazilian visa was not an easy task for John because he was Jewish. Back in those days, the Brazilian government, under the Getúlio Vargas' administration was antisemitic.

Getting a Brazilian visa was not an easy task for John because he was Jewish. Back in those days, the Brazilian government, under the Getúlio Vargas' administration was antisemitic. One of John's cousins at that time was the Director of the Biological Institute in the State of Minas Gerais, whose governor was Juscelino Kubitschek. John's cousin explained the situation to the governor, who gave him his card with his recommendations, so that a visa would be issued. John's cousin then went to Rio de Janeiro and also asked for the help of one of his wife's uncles, who was a senator and could facilitate the process at the Ministry of Foreign Affairs.

When they showed Kubitschek's card at the Ministry, one of the clerks finally revealed what was happening. "You see, your cousin's visa is on hold because he's Jewish," he explained. John's cousin could not believe his ears. "Well, I am Jewish and I am the Director of the Biological Institute of Minas Gerais, so I cannot understand what's going on here!" he replied. The clerk did not know what to do and said it had all been a mistake. Without any excuses left, the clerk finally issued John's visa.

John was unaware of the great lengths his family had gone to make it possible for him to come to Brazil. Had he known about it before, he said he would never have gone to Brazil. Many Jews had a similar experience when they decided to move there. President Getúlio Vargas had an antisemitic behavior, modelled after that of Benito Mussolini, the Italian dictator who had been a Nazi ally during World War II, as well as being a sympathizer of Hitler himself. Back then, if Jews wanted to go to Brazil, they would either have to pay to get in or be baptized and converted to Catholicism.

> **Back then, if Jews wanted to come to Brazil, they would either have to pay or be baptized and converted to Catholicism.**

As John's then girlfriend, I could not just cross the Atlantic and move to Brazil with him, so our romance developed through letters which we kept writing to each other. There were many, many letters written during the time we spent apart, which John and I have kept with the most affection. As our relationship grew stronger, John expressed his wishes to marry me in one of his letters, dated April 1953. I really liked him, but I was a little afraid of the idea of getting married and having a family. Who could ever guarantee that the same thing that happened to me would not happen to my children one day? I could not bear going through that again.

After overcoming my fear, I decided that it was exactly what I wanted to do: I wanted to marry John Konig. In order to do so, I would also need a Brazilian visa, since John was working in that country and we would start our new life there as a family. I had to go back to Holland to make arrangements for my official departure. In Amsterdam, my guardian told me that I would have to be in good standing with the Income Tax Bureau. He had prepared a dossier about my case, which was not an easy task. Then I went to the Brazilian Consulate to apply for a visa and hope it would be issued in no time.

I did not succeed on my first attempt. Later I bought a nice box of chocolates for a secretary who later introduced me to the consul. He said he could help me, but there was a chance it would take up to six months before I could get my visa. He would take my case to the Court in the Hague, since someone owed him a favor there—that would expedite the process. The consul actually asked me to go out with him, but I shut him down right away, while still keeping tabs on how things were going. I got the visa six weeks later and was free to move to a new continent with my future husband. Still, I was instructed not to fill in anything about religion in the paperwork, so as to avoid any issues.

Once I got my visa, everything was settled: I was going to get married and start a new life in a completely foreign land, where I did not know anyone besides my future husband and his relatives. When I returned to London, I started looking for a simple wedding dress. John had kept his mother's veil, which was to become a family tradition since that same veil has been used since by every bride in the family.

John and I had a civil wedding in July 1953 and our ceremony at the synagogue was performed soon after, in early August. I insisted on paying for all expenses, a decision I still regret to this day, because my uncle wanted to pay for the ceremony as a gift to me. I was too proud and did not accept it, because I really did not want anybody's help.

After I put the veil on and was about to step into the synagogue, my aunt took one look at me, removed her own pearl earrings and handed them to me. "Put them on. Otherwise, nobody will know there's a bride behind that veil," she said. When I arrived at the synagogue and saw no one there from my immediate family, it was as if everything that had happened was flashing before my eyes—everything I had lost, everyone I loved who was not there to share that moment with me. I was in shock, and that same thought kept circling in my head. *Why are you doing it? Why would you want to have a family? Just so you can lose everyone again?* However, when I saw John waiting for me at the bema—the altar of synagogues—I realized I was in good hands and could trust him.

When I arrived at the synagogue and saw no one there from my immediate family, it was as if everything that had happened was flashing before my eyes—everything I had lost, everyone I loved who was not there to share that moment with me.

It was very sad to celebrate my wedding without my parents and my brother. I really missed them in such an important moment of my life. Still, I was anxious to start a new phase in a completely new place, where memories of Bergen-Belsen and World War II would be more distant.

After our wedding in England, we returned to Holland to throw a party for the few relatives and friends I still had there and also so I could see my guardians again. Besides, I needed to go to the Central Bank to pick up the documents I needed in order to emigrate, which I was only able to get one day before we left, a few minutes before the bank closed that day. I was so tired of everything that had happened at that bank and in Holland that, as soon as I put my hands on those documents, I swore to myself never to set foot in the country again.

After celebrating my wedding in Holland and being able to get my paperwork straightened out, John and I moved to Brazil, eager to start a new life in a new country. I was going to a place where I would not have anyone but my husband and his family, but it was also a place without Westerbork, Bergen-Belsen, or any of the bitter memories of a Nazi occupation.

I did not honor my word, though. I did set foot in Holland again. Eight years after my departure, I would go back to my native land. My guardian was very upset with my absence after all those years. "I never did anything to you," he said.

That moment I realized he was right, because I did not treat him with the respect that he deserved. Even though we wrote to each other regularly, I did take too long to go and see him.

Being in a new place meant starting anew. The wounds left by the horrors I had been through would never heal though. I would never be able to forget what had happened to me. That deep pain was something that I would never be able to ignore. The absence of my family would be felt forever, and the family I would have of my own would not erase the ashes left by the Holocaust. The Holocaust was part of my history, and I could never leave it behind.

10

STARTING OVER

Life in post-war Europe was not easy. The entire continent had been devastated by battles and was trying to get back on its feet. Not only building and bridges were being rebuilt, as it happened in Holland; daily lives were being rebuilt after millions of people perished during the conflict and the fate of survivors was forever altered.

John and I were trying to build a new life away from all the losses we had to face in Europe. I had been knocked down by the Holocaust and John had lost his parents to cancer. If we had a family in Europe, our ghosts would always be around. Even though I knew I could never get away from them, starting over somewhere new was indeed a relief.

When we arrived in São Paulo, Brazil, my husband already had a job at a company. Leaving England also meant that I would have to leave my job at the bank, since now my priority would be the family we were creating together. I did not have plans to go back to work any time soon. Our story in Brazil would really bring a fresh start. Our first daughter, Elizabeth Helene, was born in June 1954.

When you have your first child, it is completely normal to feel insecure before a new world that is being unveiled before you, considering the heavy responsibilities you are taking. I wish I could have had my mother around at the time, so she could give me advice and welcome me into motherhood. However, that would never happen and I would need to learn it all on my own.

Living in Brazil was no easy task, because John's salary alone had supported the three of us and inflation was rampant. He then was invited to work at a multinational corporation in New York, so we moved to the US in December 1956, determined to start again in North America. Our second daughter, Judith Marion, was born in there in September 1957, but soon we would need to move again because of John's work. In January 1959, we went to Argentina, where we lived for brief five months.

Living in Argentina was no easy task either. Prior to our arrival, in 1955, President Juan Domingo Perón had been deposed by a coup, seeking exile in Paraguay and later moving to Spain. Argentina was politically unstable when we arrived, and politics can heavily influence people's lives—my own story was the aftermath of changes in politics and history. In May 1959 we returned to São Paulo, Brazil, where John's company opened a new factory. Our son, Martin Joseph, was born there in 1962.

After we returned to São Paulo we made no more moves and finally settled in. I soon adapted myself and started to speak Portuguese again. I remember that, when my children were little and started going to school, they thought my accent was weird. They used to say I talked with funny accent, so they asked me not to speak in front of their friends. I started to read the newspaper and underline the more difficult words, so that I could talk to them later. "Well, do you know what this word means?" I would ask them. Since they were indeed complex words, the kids did not know what they meant, but they never said I talked with a funny accent in Portuguese again.

After my children were born, I decided I would be a full-time mother, so I could take care of their education. That way, I also assured that they would never think there was something missing in our family. I knew one day they would realize there was a generation missing, though.

As I had foreseen, the inevitable happened. "Where's everyone? Why don't we have grandparents like other children do?" I tried to explain that which can never be explained, but they were not satisfied. They were actually very traumatized by our family history—they were only children, after all.

My husband's aunt, as well as my aunts from England, tried to spoil our kids with gifts and attention, but they were not exactly grandmothers. And, even though we would spend our vacation time in England, I could not say anything when they asked questions about our family being devastated, since my aunts and uncle had decided to never speak a word about concentration camps and our losses.

As my kids were growing, they started to read about the Holocaust. They did not learn anything about it at school—it was as if it had never happened, as if it had never been part of history. They did not go to Jewish schools, since John and I decided to enroll them at a British school so they would be bi-lingual. It was very hard for our family, for them, since they were only children, but they were able to overcome it.

My husband travelled a lot because of his work, therefore I was the one in charge of bringing up our children. His company offered him a position in Hong Kong, China, but he turned it down because we wanted to give our children stability and an education, instead of moving constantly. Instead of moving he found another executive position in São Paulo, where he stayed for the next 16 years.

John had a good position at the company, but we always had to manage our money. I helped him save and, for example, I would take care of everything when we would celebrate our children's birthdays, including the cake and entertainment for their guests.

Even though I was leading a happy family life, I would never be able to forget what I had experienced during those years in a concentration camp. Survivors suffer with the trauma from the moment they step outside the camp. My eating habits were forever changed due to the hardship of Bergen-Belsen. To this day, I still cannot have pasta, fried food, white bread, or anything in large quantities. Later in life, I needed to have both knees replaced as the cartilages wore away. Some doctors told me my issues were due to the malformation of bones as a consequence of my inadequate development at an age that is so crucial to human growth and development.

Even though I had suffered so much with the effects of the camp on my body, I believe the worst of the trauma is what I carry to this day in my soul.

Even though I have suffered so much with the effects of the camp on my body, I believe the worst of the trauma is what I carry to this day in my soul. I cannot forget the horrors I went through all those years. It is as if I were constantly watching a movie in my mind, unable to erase what happened.

Despite all those terrible memories, I was strong enough to keep going forward. I had to be strong to live past my nightmares and the sorrow I carry inside. All Holocaust survivors are traumatized by that terrible stage of our lives, and each one of us has to face our own ghosts. I never went back to Bergen-Belsen—I would never be able to set foot in that place.

I never went back to Bergen-Belsen—I would never be able to set foot in that place.

That was why I kept myself preoccupied, playing an active part in my children's education and taking care of the house while my husband was at work. I remember that, when the children were little, I would take them everywhere: piano lessons, swimming classes, any activities they would like to try. After they grew up and I had already become a grandma, I decided to make one of my dreams come true—which had also been one of my father's wishes: I earned my university diploma. My father wanted me to go to Law School, but I decided to study Economics instead.

In the 1980s, I was admitted at the Pontifical Catholic University in São Paulo to study towards my major. Even though I had been away from the school environment for such a long time, I studied for an entire year in order to take the entrance exam and be able to focus on the course, which only goes to show the quality education I received at home and at the Jewish School. I have always been proud of the education John and I have been able to give our children, and I was certainly inspired by what I was taught by my parents, who may have been taken away from me when I was very young, but I will always carry their legacy, their character with me.

My children were also able to lead a good life, despite the scars. The Holocaust is something that marks entire families, and there is no way one can erase something like that from one's history. My children suffered with that, my grandchildren slowly started to learn about the family trauma and my great grandchildren will eventually have to deal with it as well. There is no escaping that.

Just when I thought I had already suffered enough for a lifetime and overcome all the losses I had to face, fate brought me yet another devastating event: in 2003, I lost one of my grandsons during an avalanche in Canada, where he lived with his family. His school had organized a field trip and, in an utterly irresponsible way, they allowed students to go hiking at an extremely dangerous territory. Fourteen students left for the field trip, but only seven of them returned alive. To this day, nothing has been done about it and the school was never punished for its criminal irresponsibility.

> ***Just when I thought I had already suffered enough for a lifetime and overcome all the losses I had to face, fate brought me yet another devastating event: in 2003, I lost one of my grandsons.***

It was very hard on the entire family and everyone was affected by it. He was the son of my middle daughter, Judith Marion, and he was only fifteen. I thought I could not withstand so much pain in one lifetime and losing a son had a devastating effect on my daughter.

Judith was very shaken by the situation. "Mom, how were you able to overcome everything you had to face in your life and deal with the pain?" she asked me. I did not know what to say, because I only had to overcome what I had faced privately. After I was released from the concentration camp, nobody was interested about what Holocaust survivors had gone through—the subject was only brought up later on. Still, I believe no psychologist could have helped me understand my years in a concentration camp better than I did on my own. After all, how can you comprehend what is incomprehensible? Someone who never lived the horrors of a concentration camp can never imagine what it was like.

> ***How can you comprehend what is incomprehensible? Someone who never lived the horrors of a concentration camp can never imagine what it was like.***

I was already over sixty years old when I decided to talk about the Holocaust. My first talk was in 1999, when my granddaughter was going to college in Michigan. She thought it would be interesting if I shared my story. After that, I still took my time before becoming a speaker; it did not happen overnight.

One of the reasons that compelled me to talk about what I had gone through was the fact that few people knew what happened to Jews in Holland. There was this false belief that Holland had been a "Jewish Sanctuary"—exactly the opposite of what the occupation period and later deportations proved to be.

Holocaust is widely talked about by Polish survivors, because most of the deaths took place in Poland. Of the six million recorded deaths, about half of those individuals were Polish Jews. However, other victims must be heard as well, thus I decided to share my story.

In 2001, I went back to Holland to be reunited with survivors from the Jewish School in Amsterdam. Just like me, some survivors had been to concentration camps; others had escaped death by running away from the Nazis. During that reunion, I was reunited with Theo Coster, who later invited me to return to Holland in 2008 because he wanted to film a documentary about his story and that of his classmates. Later on, that documentary was turned into a book, *We all wore Stars: Memories of Anne Frank from her Classmates*. Not everyone agreed to participate, though; not everyone would like to revisit their past.

During that trip, when we went down memory lane to help Theo with his project, we talked a lot about our time at the Jewish School, when we became friends with Anne Frank, and also discussed our personal experiences during the Holocaust. Many were our losses during that terrible period in history. As part of the documentary, we also visited the transitional camp in Westerbork. I went there with Theo and my husband and I was surprised to see how they had transformed such a colorless landscape into a green field where children could ride their bikes. However, the smile on those children's faces could not replace the sorrow that many Dutch Jews and I had experienced there. Most of those who had been deported would never have a chance to come back and visit that place, as it was the case with my parents and my brother.

I now go to schools and colleges throughout Brazil to talk about my past. I travel a lot as part of my work. The stories I have to share are not nice, especially for me. However, I keep talking about it in the name of those who can no longer speak about it, in the name of those who lost their lives in such a brutal, incomprehensible way during the time that the Nazi doctrine was taking over Europe.

I keep talking about it in the name of those who can no longer speak about it, in the name of those who lost their lives in such a brutal, incomprehensible way during the time that the Nazi doctrine was taking over Europe.

I really enjoy speaking before an audience, especially when it is a young audience, since World War II is such a distant, abstract event for them now. Still, it has not been a century since it happened. Young people feel the impact when they see someone standing right in front of them, talking about what it was like.

I will never be able to accept and overcome what happened to me, but I will keep talking about it for the rest of my days, so that nobody can ever say that it never happened, so that the world will never forget the pain that intolerance can bring about. I dedicate my life to my struggle, and I will fight until the very end.

EPILOGUE

The Holocaust resulted in the extermination of six million Jews—innocent people who, overnight, started to be seen as criminals and had their rights stripped away. My family members are among those victims, who were unable to survive that event. I was lucky, or maybe it was indeed a miracle to survive it all to build a new reality for myself. It has not been easy; my life has been filled with trauma and difficulties I had to overcome.

Despite the losses that I have experienced throughout my journey—losing people I loved and having my home and my family property and assets taken away—I found a way to rebuild my life and find motivation to move forward. I had to be very strong to search for happiness again, but I never gave up fighting, despite the adversities. When people hear my story, they ask me if I ever felt depressed, but I tell them I did not have time for that. After all, I needed to survive.

During those three years I spent recovering at the Santpoort sanatorium in Holland, I was extremely debilitated and wondered if I would ever be able to lead a normal life again. Besides, I was still devastated after losing my family and being all alone in the world.

Still, I held my head up high and faced the facts. I never stopped fighting for my right to live and build a future of my own.

What I want the most when I share my story with a young audience is that they understand that we must always look beyond what life brings us. We will not always get to enjoy pleasant, comforting events in our lifetime, but these are challenges that can make us stronger and better prepared for the life ahead. When something bad happens to us, we cannot just give up—we must always get up and keep fighting. For example, my freedom was taken away from me for years. I was denied basic necessities and a secondary education before I had reached adulthood, but I was able to grow up in spite of it all and keep moving forward.

In sharing my story on these pages, I hope that I can help the world never forget what happened in that grim period of our history, so that people can understand that coexisting is essential to having a happy life and furthering humanity. During World War II, it was me among many other Jews who suffered. If we do not learn a lesson after that, tomorrow another group may become the victims again. I cannot allow that to happen, and that is why I wrote my story in the name of all the voices that have been silenced, including those of my parents and brother.

> ***I wrote my story in the name of all the voices that have been silenced, including those of my parents and brother.***

After spending such a long time locked away, my values changed. Simple things in life, to which I did not pay much attention, started to mean the world to me. It was a matter of basic dignity! Have you ever stopped to think what a privilege it is to have a family and a comfortable home? Having plenty of food so you do not go hungry to have a towel to dry yourself off or a warm bed to sleep at night? This all may seem so basic, and we often take it all for granted. That is why

I have something I would like to ask of you: Be happy and thankful for every simple aspect of your life, for being healthy and near your loved ones. That is enough reason to celebrate.

After what I have been through, I realized our most precious asset is freedom—the freedom to come and go, the freedom to have your beliefs, the freedom to be who you are. There is nothing more restrictive for human beings than not allowing them to be who they are. It is crucial that we value our identity. However, we must fight so that everyone can exercise their freedom as well—the kind of freedom that does not invade other people's spaces, that does not nullify others, so that we can all be free and happy as well.

I was told I was inferior because I was Jewish, but I never believed that. As they did it to the Jewish people, the Nazis imposed their superiority on different groups, including gypsies, homosexuals, the physically disabled and other minorities they believed not to be comparable to their racial purity. I never believed in the superiority of any single being compared to others, because when we take away our particular aspects as far as culture and lifestyle, we all share the same core. That is why I do not want anyone to believe they are inferior, so as to never subject themselves to others who are eager for power, so as to never lose their freedom.

I never believed in the superiority of any single being when compared to others, because when we take away our particular aspects as far as culture and life, we all share the same core.

Therefore, I wrote this book in the name of freedom and tolerance. I also wrote this book in the memory of my parents and brother, because I am aware of the injustices that led to their death, for I know that they would have done the same in my place. Due to a twist of fate, I am the one here today, and I will never allow their legacy to fade away—as well as the legacy of all those who perished during the

Holocaust. With my testimony, I want to give voice to those who have been silenced and can no longer share their stories and sorrow.

Therefore, I wrote this book in the name of freedom and tolerance.

Unfortunately, even though we often yell, "Never again!" the history of mankind continues to develop into wars—unjustified wars—that seem to forget how valuable life is. And that is why the Holocaust is still a very current topic that must be remembered forever.

It has been over seventy years since I was released from Bergen-Belsen and able to leave that camp of horrors. However, I still remember everything I went through in that prison as if it were today. In order to prevent other people from going through that same experience, I am leaving my mark in the world. I hope everyone, young and old, may enjoy a happy life and always exercise tolerance and respect towards one another.

PICTURES

Nanette as a baby.

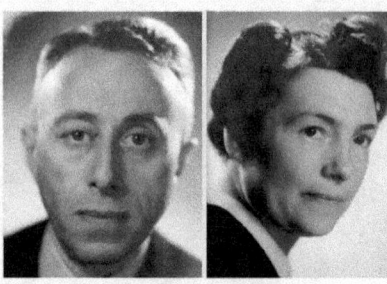

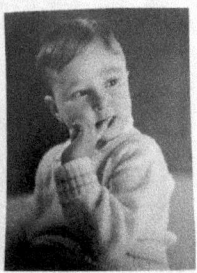

The Blitz Family had enjoyed a happy life before the war, despite the hard loss of their youngest family member, Willem, at the age of four. Above, on the left, is Nanette's father, Martijn Willem Blitz. On the right is her mother, Helene. Below, on the left, is their first born, Bernard Martijn. On the right is Willem, who was born with a heart condition.

Nanette (third row on the far right) on her annual elementary school picture, among the classmates she went to school with in her childhood.

This school book contained Nanette's memories from elementary school. The book was found and kept by her neighbors after the Blitz family was brutally taken out of their house in September 1943.

Eight-year-old Nanette (to the right of the schoolteacher) with her teachers and classmates in elementary school. Back then, schools were not segregated in Holland, so Jews and Christians could study together.

Colorful drawings by Nanette when she was nine. She was a happy child who enjoyed a calm life in Amsterdam.

Nanette (far left) and her friends wearing traditional Dutch costumes.

Above, Nanette. Below, Anne Frank. Both pictures were taken at the time they were going to Jewish school together. These pictures show slight physical similarities between the classmates. Nanette witnessed the day Anne received her famous diary as a gift and was identified as "E.S." in Anne's book.

Nanette and her family celebrating her parents Martijn Willem and Helene's anniversary. Among those present were her grandparents, uncles, and aunts, who would also suffered with the horrors of the Holocaust. Just like the Blitz family, millions of Jewish families had their lives affected by the Holocaust.

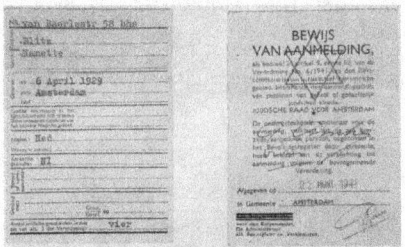

Through the Jewish Council, Nazi Germany started to impose restrictions to Dutch Jewish citizens. Nanette's documentation from March 22, 1941 identifies her as Jewish. That was her passport to the horror that was yet to come.

The yellow Star of David that Nanette had to wear in order to be identified as Jewish. She has kept it to this day.

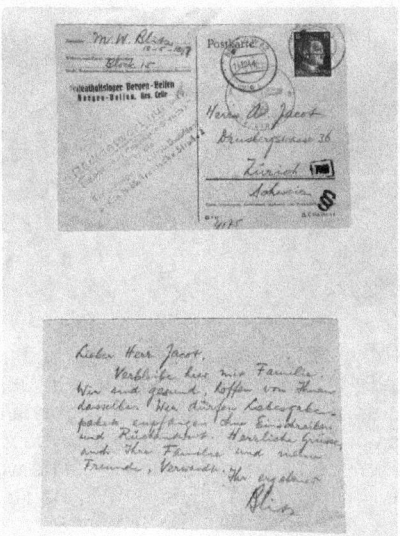

Nanette's father was allowed to send this postcard from Bergen-Belsen to a Swiss Banker, who sent it to her aunt in England. It is unknown why this was sent, perhaps he was trying to negotiate their release.

The Liberation of Bergen-Belsen Concentration Camp, April 1945. Overview of Camp No 1, taken from a watch tower used by the German guards. Picture: Wikimedia.

Unlike other SS guards, Josef Kramer did not flee before the Britain troops arrived at Bergen-Belsen, and he was arrested after explaining the condition the camp was in. He did not show any remorse regarding the lives he had taken and claimed that he was "only following orders." Picture: Wikimedia.

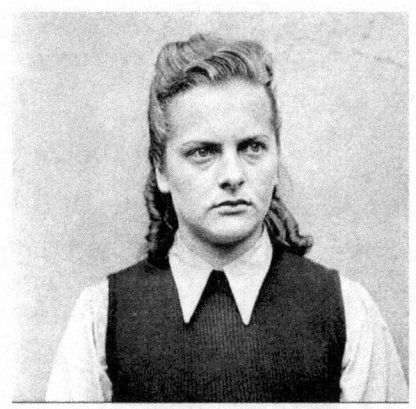

Irma Grese was one of the cruelest SS guards during the Holocaust. She was extremely feared for the abuses she had committed towards female prisoners. She was 22 when she was hanged for the atrocities she committed during World War II. Mugshot of Bergen-Belsen guard Irma Grese (1923-1945) at Celle, awaiting trial, August 1945. Picture: Wikimedia

The Liberation of Bergen-Belsen, April 1945. Wearing protective clothing, men of 11 Light Field Ambulance, Royal Army Medical Corps evacuate inmates from one of the huts at Belsen. Picture: Wikimedia.

The Liberation of Bergen-Belsen, April 1945. Overview of Camp No 1, taken from a watch tower used by the German guards. Picture: Wikimedia.

The Liberation of Bergen-Belsen April 1945. The SS camp guards are made to load the bodies of dead prisoners onto a lorry for burial. Picture: Wikimedia.

Gravestone of Anne Frank and her sister Margot Frank at Bergen-Belsen. Picture by the publisher (2017).

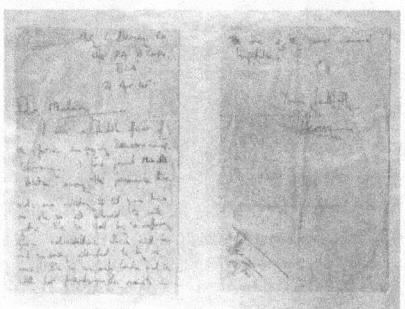

Letter written by Major Leonard Berney to Nanette's family in England on April 21, 1945: "Dear Madam, I am a British Officer of the force occupying BELSEN camp, Germany. I have found Nanette Blitz among the prisoners there, and am writing to let you know as she is not allowed to write yet. She is well but suffering from malnutrition, which will be and is being attended to by us now. She is in safe hands and is with her friends—she assists in one of the camp women's hospital. Yours faithfully, L Berney."

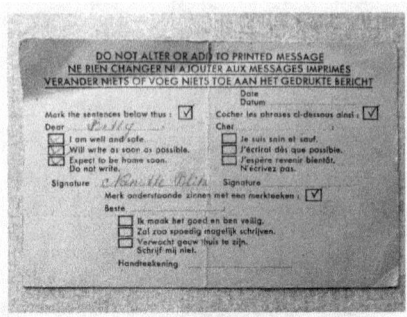

The standard letter sent to Nanette's aunt to inform her that her niece was fine.

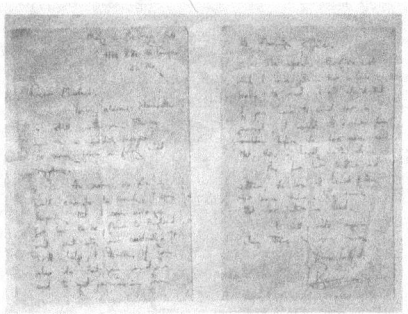

Second letter sent by Lieutenant Berney to Nanette's family in England on May 22, 1945: "Dear Madam, Your niece Nanette is still with us. She is now at a British hospital, recovering from a fairly mild typhus. As soon as she is well enough to travel, I am hoping that I can arrange for her to be flown to England and put into your custody. It will help, I think, if you could make all possible efforts to get a permission from the Foreign Office. She speaks English well and I have given her a few books to read. I am afraid that, if you care to send her a parcel, it would not arrive before she had gone, so that this is hardly worth doing. As for her brother and mother, she has not heard from them for some time. She knows her father died. I will write again when there is more news. Yours faithfully, L Berney."

Nanette's "Displaced Person" card. After the end of WWII, Europe witnessed an intense transit of survivors wishing to return to their native country.

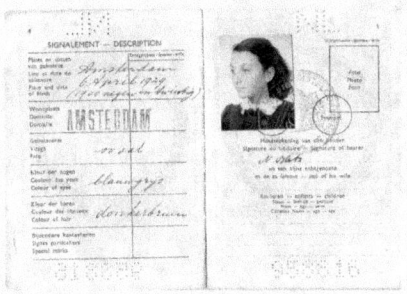

After the liberation, Nanette went back to Eindhoven, in Holland, on July 24, 1945, as shown on the passport.

Twenty-two-year-old Nanette in June 1951, in England. This picture was taken by John Konig on their first date.

Nanette and John Konig on their wedding day in August 1953.

Nanette and John Konig on their wedding day in
August 1953 (close-up).

Nanette and John on their fiftieth anniversary in Brazil,
joined by their children Martin Joseph, Elizabeth
Helene, and Judith Marion in 2003.

In 2009, a Dutch TV channel reunited Anne Frank's surviving classmates to pay tribute to her. That same year, had she been alive, Anne would have been 80 years old. The documentary was so successful that there were a few reruns. Among those present are Nanette, in the center, and Danka, in red. In 1941, Danka had told Nanette that Germans were killing Jews by asphyxiation in Poland. Back then, it was something difficult to grasp.

Nanette and her husband John.

Nanette and John in front of gravestone at Muiderberg cemetery (The Netherlands) for family killed in the Holocaust.

KIND REVIEW REQUEST

It is my sincere hope that you have enjoyed reading my story. It would be very much appreciated if you could possibly leave a short review.
That would help getting more exposure for my memoirs.

I still read all reviews!

Many thanks in advance,
Nanette (b. 1929)

AMSTERDAM PUBLISHERS HOLOCAUST LIBRARY

The series **Holocaust Survivor Memoirs World War II** consists of the following autobiographies of survivors:

Hank Brodt Holocaust Memoirs. A Candle and a Promise, by Deborah Donnelly

The Dead Years. Holocaust Memoirs, by Joseph Schupack

Rescued from the Ashes. The Diary of Leokadia Schmidt, Survivor of the Warsaw Ghetto, by Leokadia Schmidt

My Lvov. Holocaust Memoir of a twelve-year-old Girl, by Janina Hescheles

Remembering Ravensbrück. From Holocaust to Healing, by Natalie Hess

Wolf. A Story of Hate, by Zeev Scheinwald with Ella Scheinwald

Save my Children. An Astonishing Tale of Survival and its Unlikely Hero, by Leon Kleiner with Edwin Stepp

Holocaust Memoirs of a Bergen-Belsen Survivor & Classmate of Anne Frank, by Nanette Blitz Konig

Defiant German - Defiant Jew. A Holocaust Memoir from inside the Third Reich, by Walter Leopold with Les Leopold

In a Land of Forest and Darkness. The Holocaust Story of two Jewish Partisans, by Sara Lustigman Omelinski

Holocaust Memories. Annihilation and Survival in Slovakia, by Paul Davidovits

From Auschwitz with Love. The Inspiring Memoir of Two Sisters' Survival, Devotion and Triumph Told by Manci Grunberger Beran & Ruth Grunberger Mermelstein, by Daniel Seymour

Remetz. Resistance Fighter and Survivor of the Warsaw Ghetto, by Jan Yohay Remetz

My March Through Hell. A Young Girl's Terrifying Journey to Survival, by Halina Kleiner with Edwin Stepp

———————

The series **Holocaust Survivor True Stories WWII** consists of the following biographies:

Among the Reeds. The true story of how a family survived the Holocaust, by Tammy Bottner

A Holocaust Memoir of Love & Resilience. Mama's Survival from Lithuania to America, by Ettie Zilber

Living among the Dead. My Grandmother's Holocaust Survival Story of Love and Strength, by Adena Bernstein Astrowsky

Heart Songs. A Holocaust Memoir, by Barbara Gilford

Shoes of the Shoah. The Tomorrow of Yesterday, by Dorothy Pierce

Hidden in Berlin. A Holocaust Memoir, by Evelyn Joseph Grossman

Separated Together. The Incredible True WWII Story of Soulmates Stranded an Ocean Apart, by Kenneth P. Price, Ph.D.

The Man Across the River. The incredible story of one man's will to survive the Holocaust, by Zvi Wiesenfeld

If Anyone Calls, Tell Them I Died. A Memoir, by Emanuel (Manu) Rosen

The House on Thrömerstrasse. A Story of Rebirth and Renewal in the Wake of the Holocaust, by Ron Vincent

Dancing with my Father. His hidden past. Her quest for truth. How Nazi Vienna shaped a family's identity, by Jo Sorochinsky

The Story Keeper. Weaving the Threads of Time and Memory - A Memoir, by Fred Feldman

Krisia's Silence. The Girl who was not on Schindler's List, by Ronny Hein

Defying Death on the Danube. A Holocaust Survival Story, by Debbie J. Callahan with Henry Stern

A Doorway to Heroism. A decorated German-Jewish Soldier who became an American Hero, by Rabbi W. Jack Romberg

The Shoemaker's Son. The Life of a Holocaust Resister, by Laura Beth Bakst

The Redhead of Auschwitz. A True Story, by Nechama Birnbaum

Land of Many Bridges. My Father's Story, by Bela Ruth Samuel Tenenholtz

Creating Beauty from the Abyss. The Amazing Story of Sam Herciger, Auschwitz Survivor and Artist, by Lesley Ann Richardson

On Sunny Days We Sang. A Holocaust Story of Survival and Resilience, by Jeannette Grunhaus de Gelman

Painful Joy. A Holocaust Family Memoir, by Max J. Friedman

I Give You My Heart. A True Story of Courage and Survival, by Wendy Holden

In the Time of Madmen, by Mark A. Prelas

Monsters and Miracles. Horror, Heroes and the Holocaust, by Ira Wesley Kitmacher

Flower of Vlora. Growing up Jewish in Communist Albania, by Anna Kohen

Aftermath: Coming of Age on Three Continents. A Memoir, by Annette Libeskind Berkovits

Not a real Enemy. The True Story of a Hungarian Jewish Man's Fight for Freedom, by Robert Wolf

Zaidy's War. Four Armies, Three Continents, Two Brothers. One Man's Impossible Story of Endurance, by Martin Bodek

The Glassmaker's Son. Looking for the World my Father left behind in Nazi Germany, by Peter Kupfer

The Apprentice of Buchenwald. The True Story of the Teenage Boy Who Sabotaged Hitler's War Machine, by Oren Schneider

The Cello Still Sings. A Generational Story of the Holocaust and of the Transformative Power of Music, by Janet Horvath

———

The series **Jewish Children in the Holocaust** consists of the following autobiographies of Jewish children hidden during WWII in the Netherlands:

Searching for Home. The Impact of WWII on a Hidden Child, by Joseph Gosler

See You Tonight and Promise to be a Good Boy! War memories, by Salo Muller

Sounds from Silence. Reflections of a Child Holocaust Survivor, Psychiatrist and Teacher, by Robert Krell

Sabine's Odyssey. A Hidden Child and her Dutch Rescuers, by Agnes Schipper

The Journey of a Hidden Child, by Harry Pila with Robin Black

---

The series **New Jewish Fiction** consists of the following novels, written by Jewish authors. All novels are set in the time during or after the Holocaust.

The Corset Maker. A Novel, by Annette Libeskind Berkovits

Escaping the Whale. The Holocaust is over. But is it ever over for the next generation? by Ruth Rotkowitz

When the Music Stopped. Willy Rosen's Holocaust, by Casey Hayes

Hands of Gold. One Man's Quest to Find the Silver Lining in Misfortune, by Roni Robbins

The Girl Who Counted Numbers. A Novel, by Roslyn Bernstein

There was a garden in Nuremberg. A Novel, by Navina Michal Clemerson

The Butterfly and the Axe, by Omer Bartov

Good for a Single Journey, by Helen Joyce

The series **Holocaust Books for Young Adults** consists of the following novels, based on true stories:

The Boy behind the Door. How Salomon Kool Escaped the Nazis. Inspired by a True Story, by David Tabatsky

Running for Shelter. A True Story, by Suzette Sheft

The Precious Few. An Inspirational Saga of Courage based on True Stories, by David Twain with Art Twain

Jacob's Courage: A Holocaust Love Story, by Charles S. Weinblatt

---

Want to be an AP book reviewer?

Reviews are very important in a world dominated by the social media and social proof. Please drop us a line if you want to join the *AP review team.* We will then add you to our list of advance reviewers. No strings attached, and we promise that we will not be spamming you.

info@amsterdampublishers.com